Chris Green

W9-CPE-709

What's Your Problem?

Posing and Solving Mathematical Problems, K–2

Penny Skinner

HEINEMANN
Portsmouth, NH

For my father, Peter Sharp, and my sister,
Deborah Rudder, thanking them for their interest.

HEINEMANN EDUCATIONAL BOOKS, INC.
361 Hanover Street   Portsmouth, NH 03801
Offices and agents throughout the world.

First published in 1990 by
THOMAS NELSON AUSTRALIA
102 Dodds Street
South Melbourne, Victoria 3205

First published in the United States in 1991 by Heinemann.
91 92 93 94 95   5 4 3 2 1

©Penny Skinner, 1990

All rights reserved. No part of this publication may be reproduced
in any form without prior permission of the publisher.

Library of Congress Cataloging-in-Publication Data

Skinner, Penny.
      What's your problem? : posing and solving mathematical problems,
K-2/Penny Skinner.
         p.   cm.
      "First published in 1990 by Thomas Nelson Australia"—T.p. verso.
      ISBN 0-435-08326-0. — ISBN 0-17-007686-5
      1. Mathematics—Study and teaching (Primary)   2. Problem solving.
I. Title.
QA135.5.S55   1991
372.7—dc20   91-20373
                                                       CIP

Cover design by Jenny Jensen Greenleaf
Designed by Karen Harbour
Typeset in 11/13 Italia and Avant Garde by The Type Gallery, Melbourne
Printed in The United States of America

Contents

Preface

This book describes the progress over two and a half years of one class of children in a problem-centred mathematics program.

I taught the class from midway through their Kindergarten year in 1985 until the end of 1987 at Macgregor Primary School in the A.C.T.

In outlining here how the program developed I hope to provide information that may help other teachers establish their own programs.

The program can be used in conjunction with any mathematics curriculum for its central concern is teaching style, not content. The teaching emphasis is upon the presentation of mathematical concepts and skills through problems, many of which should be generated by the children themselves.

Introduction

As problems are central to "real world" mathematics and, I believe, to effective learning, I made them the focus of the mathematics program described in this book.

What is a problem?

There is some debate in educational circles as to what constitutes a problem. Before embarking on my program I established a working definition of a problem.

I considered the many types of mathematical problems that people encounter outside schools. They range from simple "How many?", "How much?" and "How big?" problems to more complex ones involving extensive investigation. An essential aspect of each problem is that the person attempting to solve it needs or wants to do so. This became the premise for the program. The children were involved and engaged by the problems. They wanted to solve them.

My definition of a problem, stated most simply, is this:

> **A problem is a question which engages someone in searching for a solution.**

This definition implies two essential conditions of a problem:

- A problem cannot exist separately from the person who *poses* and *solves* it. Posing problems is as important as solving them. A feature of "real world" problems is that they are usually solved by the person who has posed them. Thus they fully engage the problem solver.
- The problem-solver has to *search* for a way to find a solution. A problem is not simply answered by memory recall. The children and I have a set of potential problems, each one written as a story in book form. One child aptly called them "trouble books". Problem-solvers have to go to some trouble to find answers. One of my books poses this problem:

Tim has chicken pox. He has five spots on each leg, and five spots on each arm, and five spots on his tummy. How many chicken pox spots does Tim have?

When the kindergarten children read this problem, they had to work out a way to solve it. Some of them asked the real Tim in the class to lie on the floor while they put red counters on his arms, legs and tummy. Tim was not too happy about this strategy, and the counters rolled off his body as he protested. The children had to devise more successful strategies. Corinne drew around Tim as he lay on a length of paper. Lisa said, "You can draw a little picture of Tim and put dots on it". Tim himself wrote the numeral 5 five times and said, "You can just count in fives ... 5, 10, 15, 20, 25".

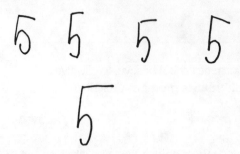

A wide range of types of questions can form the basis of a problem. Even a question like, "How many toy animals are here?" is a problem if it fulfills the two conditions described.

"Real world" problems

Because "real world" problems form the basis of my definition, they thereby fulfill the two conditions of what constitutes a problem. Teachers need to be alert to any real mathematical problems that arise and allow the children to work out their own ways to solve them.

"How many writing pencils do we need to order?"

"How can we cut the birthday cake into thirty pieces?"

"How shall we divide the class into teams?"

"What rules do we need for this game?"

Contrived problems

To ensure a balance in mathematical content it is sometimes necessary to provide contrived problems. In using contrived problems, there is the danger that the problem-solver has no real purpose in solving them and thus is not engaged by them. The use of contrived problems that appear in teacher resource books is often merely gimmicky. They can indeed become useful problems, but only if adopted by the problem-solver for some purpose beyond satisfying a teacher's requirements.

In this program, the contrived problems and those found in resource books were useful as starting points for the children's work. They were used to introduce ideas or as the basis for discussion. The children often extended these problems by posing related ones. Many contrived problems were presented in book form so the children could work on them in their own time.

Contrived problems as a starting point

Brady and Philip are working with the problem books at quiet reading time. The one they are reading begins with three carrots, so the boys have put out three orange Unifix cubes to represent the carrots.

These problems were useful because they motivated the children to write their own problem books and they presented a range of problem structures.

The children's problems

The most common type of problem the children posed was the story problem which involved operating on numbers.

Amber wrote the following problem.

There was a gang of robbers. The robbers broke into a bank. They stole all the money. They left 50 fingerprints on the safe. How many robbers were there?

Amber's problem was shared with the class later in the day.

The children produced problems in response to many curriculum areas. Topics dealt with in science, social studies, art and literature gave the children ideas for problems. One group wrote the following "poem" that became a problem:

> The 11 little girls.
> There were 11 little pillows they
> found 11 little beds. They lay
> down on the 11 little beds.
> Along came 11 little girls and
> lay in the 11 little beds. And
> had 11 little dreams.
> They dreamed of 11 little pets.
>
> How many all together?

Solving problems

The children's story problems engaged the class in problem solving activity as the children were keenly interested in each other's work. They gave each other feedback on the appropriateness of the problems, and they extended each other's ideas.

At first most of the children's story problems involved simple addition, multiplication, subtraction and division. The problem solvers had to determine which operations to use and how to apply them effectively. When the children worked on the problems, they mostly used concrete materials such as Unifix cubes and MAB blocks. They constantly refined their strategies for using such materials. For instance, early strategies included grouping the Unifix cubes in tens, placing the Unifix cubes or MAB blocks (wooden blocks based on a unit measurement of one cubic centimetre, similar to Dienes blocks or Base 10 blocks) in ordered arrangements rather than haphazardly, and exchanging "tens" and "ones".

The children's problems grew in complexity and required more sophisticated solutions. Over time, they found written calculations helpful in solving problems.

Some problems required the children to do some research. Here are two examples:

There were 4 dinosaurs in days of long ago.
Heptaceratops   uniceratops
Pentaceratops   triceratops
How many horns altogether?

The martian ate all of Jupiter's moons
and all Africa's Deserts.

how many things did the martian eat?

Other problems led to quite extensive investigations, like this one from Craig:

27/10/87

To Mrs Skinner,
          Here is a problem for the class to do on the calculaters. And this is true. playschool is 21 years old. And there's two shows a day. One show by itself is half-an-hour. I want to find out how many hours it would be all together. but! if there's 365 day's in a year (not including a leap year) playschool only on from Monday-Friday so how do you work it out?
          from Craig

p.s I've allready worked it out

Realising the potential of contrived problems

The children's problems did not cover all curriculum topics so it was necessary to find a way to introduce them. Contrived problems were used as a starting point and I encouraged the children to extend them.

When using a contrived problem I often pretended I was making it up and thus modelled problem posing. By my giving reasons for posing each problem the children felt encouraged to contribute ideas.

The topic of odd and even numbers illustrates how the children adopted and extended contrived problems. The children had already investigated what odd and even numbers were before commencing this work.

A group of children wrote a story which began: "A building is on fire! Here comes the fire engine! Here comes the fireman! The fireman is climbing a ladder."

I recalled a problem I had read elsewhere and used it to extend the children's story. Before writing, I explained to the class that I was going to make up some clues about the size of the ladder. The clues were:

He is on the middle rung of the ladder. He goes up three more steps to get to the top of the ladder. How many rungs are on the ladder?

We made our story into an illustrated book and the children devised ways to work out the answer to the problem. Alison used straws for the rungs of the ladder.

The children extended the problem by changing the number of rungs on the ladder and then making up some clues of their own but always starting with the firemen on the middle rung. Several children noted the ladder always had an odd number of rungs and we discussed why this was so.

Some time later I read to the class A.A. Milne's poem "Halfway down", in which a child sits on the middle stair of a staircase. One child asked how many stairs there were in the staircase and the class then investigated how many there might be.

Some children made models of staircases. Teresa's is pictured overleaf.

Some children drew staircases, like these ones by Shannon and Cameron.

It is an odd number. But not one.

In a follow-up discussion the children concluded that there could be any odd number of stairs except one, because you cannot have a middle stair if there is an even number of stairs, or if there is only one. The children looked at the illustration in the A.A. Milne book which shows a child sitting on a stair, the stairs above that one, but not the stairs below. The picture reminded some of them about the fireman's ladder problem and we discussed the relationship between the two situations.

I asked the children if they could pose any other problems about odd numbers. This led them to pose problems focusing on the addition of odd and even numbers:

- What happens if you add two odd numbers?
- What happens if you add three odd numbers?
- What happens if you add any odd number of odd numbers?
- What happens if you add two even numbers?
- What happens if you add one even number and one odd number?

These questions formed the basis of investigations like this one:

| Odd + evens. | Kate

What happens when you add an odd and an even?

1+2=3
3+2=5
65+4=69.
So far they equal an odd number.
103+6=109
This time for shore odd numbers plus even numbers equal odd numbers.

The class then posed the following problem related to odd and even numbers:

Fold a sheet of paper down the middle. With a hole puncher, punch holes through both layers of paper. Open up the paper. Do you think you have an even number of holes or an odd number of holes? Check.

Some children found that by punching a hole at the very edge of the fold they could make an odd number of holes. They added to our problem:

How can you make an odd number of holes? Because it is possible.

David wrote a problem based on experiments he had done with lengths of yarn:

Fold a piece of yarn in the middle and make two layers like this:

Now cut through BOTH layers as many times as you like. Now count your pieces. Will there be an odd number or an even number?

Games

Many of the children's investigations inspired them to make games. Our work on odd and even numbers led Renee to make a game called Noah's Ark. She made a wooden boat and used planks of wood for a river. She put the boat on the river and installed a ramp leading up to the boat. She marked the ramp into sections. Next she got some Unifix cubes and called them animals. Her idea was for two players each to choose an animal and proceed up the ramp onto the boat. The first player to land an animal on the boat was the winner. To determine how to proceed up the ramp, Renee decided to use a twenty-sided die. The players took turns to throw the die. If they threw an even number they could move one step up the ramp. If they threw an odd number they would end up in the river. These rules frustrated the players as they always ended up in the river. Renee therefore amended the rules so that when an odd number was thrown, the animal simply stayed where it was.

With the failure of the early rule whereby the animal fell into the river when an odd number was thrown, Renee and her friends diverged into investigating aspects of probability.

Later we changed the game so that two regular dice were used. If the combination of the numbers on the two faces was odd, then the animal would remain still. If the combination was even, then the animal would move up the ramp. This reinforced what the children found out about adding two odd numbers.

The children helped me make another game based on their work with odd and even numbers. It is called "The Spot Box game" and had its beginnings in a book we read, *Put me in the Zoo* by Robert Lopshire, (Random House, 1966). There is a "spot box" in the story and the spots jump around from one object to another. Our spot box game has two "animals", which are simply two squares of felt; forty cardboard circles, which are the "spots"; and an ordinary die. Two players each lay out an animal and pick up an odd number of spots (the same number each). They then take it in turns to throw the die and put their spots onto their animal according to the number thrown; a condition is that an animal can only have an odd number of spots at any time. The winner is the first player to get all his or her spots on their animal.

Mathematics concepts and skills

As the children solved problems and worked on investigations, they developed a wide range of mathematical concepts and skills. Within a purposeful context, they competently measured and calculated.

They devised ways to add, subtract, multiply and divide. They were proficient at mental calculations and they came to find written algorithms an effective alternative to the use of concrete materials. Written number work was not a separate entity in the program. Whenever it arose it was in the context of problem solving and investigation.

Thus the children gained the skills traditionally taught in school mathematics programs, and much more as well.

ORGANISATION

1.1 Organising content

Content overview

The following content overview chart shows the curriculum framework that formed the basis of this program for the first three years of school.

	Kindergarten (5-to-6 year olds)
Classification	• Making collections • Labelling • Numbers as labels
Counting	• Number names to twenty • Rhythmic counting • Estimating up to ten objects
Understanding numbers	• Grouping in numbers less than ten, e.g. base three grouping
Symbolism	• Exploring general symbolism concepts • Numerals 1–10
Posing problems	• Posing story problems (addition and subtraction) • Setting investigation topics
Solving problems	• Problems involving the four operations • Acting out problems • Making models of problems • Pictures and diagrams of problems
Pattern	• Regular patterns • Repeating patterns
Investigating numbers	• Finding out about numbers to ten through pattern making • Representing patterns in a variety of ways
Concrete computation	• Solving problems with concrete materials • Finger maths
Mental computation	• Recalling number patterns
Written computation	• Exploring the use of pencil and paper to make calculations (pictures)
Investigating measurement	• Comparative measurement
Investigating space	• Position • Building with three-dimensional shapes • Deriving two-dimensional shapes from the faces of three-dimensional shapes • Describing and naming circles, squares, triangles and rectangles

Year one (6-to-7 year olds)	Year two (7-to-8 year olds)
• Classification as an investigation technique	• Hierarchical classification
• Counting in groups, e.g counting in twos • Grouping in tens • Exploring different ways to count • Estimating quantities to about thirty	• Grouping in hundreds and thousands • Estimating up to about a hundred • Rounding numbers
• Base ten grouping • Place value (tens and ones) • Money as a number system	• Place value (hundreds and thousands)
• Operation symbols • Investigating calculators	→
• Story problems featuring all operations • Shared writing of puzzle problems • Increasing responsibility for setting investigation topics	• Story problems featuring a range of concepts, e.g. fractions, measurement, money, time • Abstract number problems
• Working systematically • Developing a repertoire of problem-solving strategies	→
• Sequences of numbers • Odd and even numbers • Staircase (triangular) numbers • Square numbers • Rectangular arrangements of numbers	• Three-dimensional pattern work with numbers, e.g. cubic numbers, pyramid numbers
• Investigating number relationships • Writing reports • Using number sentences to record findings	→
• Using MAB blocks • Grouping blocks • Exchanging tens and ones • Doubling and halving strategies	• Using materials where place value is denoted by position, e.g. loop abacus • Combining steps when calculating
• Addition and subtraction strategies • Memorising some addition facts	• Multiplication and division strategies • Memorising some multiplication facts
• Visual representation of numbers	• Vertical addition and subtraction of two- and three-digit numbers
• Making comparisons with informal units of measurement • Standardising informal units • Telling the time on a one-handed analogue clock • Digital time	• Standard units of measurement • Estimating measurement • Telling the time on a two-handed analogue clock
• Making, classifying and naming polygons • Computer Logo • Symmetry	• Classifying, describing and naming three-dimensional shapes • Relationships between two-dimensional shapes

The school curriculum

As this program is essentially concerned with teaching style rather than with content, it can be used in conjunction with any set curriculum.

When I developed the program, I had to work within my school's mathematics curriculum. I began by listing all the topics to be covered in that year.

These formed the basis of this problem-oriented program. I noted on my list the curriculum topics which the children were spontaneously covering as they generated problems and investigations.

The children did not spontaneously cover all the topics set in the curriculum so some had to be initiated by posing problems, using contrived problems and setting investigation topics. With a bit of planning, no matter what the set curriculum, all topics can be presented through problems and investigations.

Programming

As the program featured children generating a lot of work, all planning had to reflect this. The amount of detail in the planning varied according to how much work the children were generating.

In Kindergarten and at the beginning of each following year, each mathematics session was planned in detail. The children were involved as much as possible by encouraging them to suggest ideas both for investigation topics and for problems we could prepare together.

Since developing the program with one class, I have put it into practice with a Year One class and a composite Year One/Two. At the outset of each year I did detailed planning to establish the routines of problem writing, problem sharing and investigations. The introduction of mathematics games was also carefully planned so the children clearly understood each one's purpose and procedure.

A range of investigation topics encompassing measurement, space, statistics, classification and number was also planned. In this way the children became aware of the range of possibilities for their own topic choices.

As much as possible I used the children's ideas as the basis for these early sessions. When Hayley brought to school a Lego model she had made which showed fifteen as a triangular number, we tackled the topic, "Finding out about numbers with Lego".

The problems the children wrote were used to introduce topics. For instance, in Year One, Jenny wrote a problem requiring the addition of the legs of various animals. After the problem was shared with the class I asked if I could keep the problem book for the next day's session. On the next day we reread the problem and I asked, "What's interesting about the number of legs each animal has? Let's see if we can find out." The children found that all animals with legs have an even number of them and we discussed why that was so. They also found that half the legs were on one side of the body and half were on the other side, which led to some work on symmetry. Of course they also found other facts, such as that birds have two legs and insects have six.

As each year progressed the children took increasing responsibility for setting their own mathematics topics, so I needed to do less planning than I had earlier in the year. Occasionally, when the children were lacking ideas, they needed help in developing new directions.

1.2 Organising time

A daily timetable

I programmed a block session each day for mathematics, in between the recess and lunch breaks. The first session each day was spent on language and the afternoon session was spent on reading, music, drama, art, science, social studies and P.E. This timetabling was very flexible as all subjects were integrated.

Mathematics also occurred incidentally during the day outside the block session. During the morning language session children often wrote on mathematics topics. At reading time each afternoon, they often chose to work with the problem books. A music and movement lesson or an art lesson might have been based on number patterns.

In the daily mathematics block session, P.E., art, music, science, and social science were sometimes integrated. For instance, we might have investigated a P.E. topic such as, "Find the three quickest ways to get from one end of the basketball court to the other".

Planning a mathematics session

Most mathematics sessions followed a pattern like this:

Problem sharing	20 – 30 minutes
Investigation	20 – 50 minutes
Games	up to 35 minutes
Sharing the children's investigative work and following it up	20 – 30 minutes

The time for each activity varied according to the age of the children and the topic under investigation. The longer the time taken on the investigation, the less time remained for games, and on some days there was no time for games. As each child completed work on an investigation, he or she played a game (see the Introduction, and Chapters 5, 7 and 8).

1.3 Organising evaluation

Monitoring children's progress

I kept a written record of the progress of each child. These were based on observations of the children working, on the problems they wrote, and on regular structured "maths chats" with each individual child. These were kept in unlined exercise books, one for each child.

Maths chats

I had a maths chat with each child, lasting from five to ten minutes, once every two or three weeks. These sessions were conducted while the class worked on investigations or played mathematics games.

During these sessions I set problems and suggested investigation topics so that I could assess the children's progress in developing concepts, problem-solving strategies, investigation strategies and computation skills. As the children worked, I encouraged them to discuss with me what they were doing and how they were thinking.

April

T: Do you have a favourite number?

L: 6, because I'm 6. And one, because you can turn an odd number into an even number if you add one.

T: What happens if you add one to an even number?

L: It makes it odd! (No hesitation)

T: Let's pretend you're a twin and you're turning 7. Your dad makes you each a birthday cake.

L: He's got to get 14 candles!

T: How do you know that?

L: I just know 7 and 7 is 14.

T: Why are 7 and 7 14?

L: ... 7, and 3 from the other 7 is 10 and there's 4 left. So it's 14.

T: Well, Dad goes shopping to buy candles, and the packs have 12 candles in them. What will he do?

L: He gets 2 packs. And he'll have some spares.

T: If he uses the spares for your next birthday, how many more will he need to buy?

L: There's 10 spares ... (She puts out 8 MAB ones, then another 8) Look, 4 and 4 and 4 and 4. (She arranges them in a square and counts them) 16. It's a square number. 8 and 8 are 16. We have to have 16 candles next year ...

T: How many packets will Dad buy?

L: Well, there's 10 spares this year ... 1 more pack. And he'll have more spares!

An extract from Lisa's progress record.

I sometimes asked the children to use specific materials (e.g. pencil and paper) so I could observe how they used them.

Concepts

The problems I set focused on the concepts listed in the school's mathematics curriculum. I always extended a basic question by discussing the children's responses with them. For instance, in order to see what the children understood about the relative sizes of fractions, I asked questions like "Would you rather have a third of a chocolate cake or a sixth?" "A sixth", one child replied to that question. I assumed he thought that a sixth was a larger fraction than a third; but when I asked him why, he replied "Because if I had a third I would probably be sick". First assumptions are not always accurate, and should be clarified by discussion.

Counting

I would put a number of Unifix cubes in front of the child, or draw a number of circles on a piece of paper and ask, "How many are there?" I would ask the child to make two estimates first.

I noted the relationship between the two estimates and their appropriateness. A great difference between the two estimates indicated that the child was guessing, rather than using a strategy. From the beginning, I encouraged the children to estimate, as it would help them form visual models of numbers. Useful strategies included estimating how many pairs of objects there were, looking for patterns such as three threes or two fours, and estimating how many tens there were.

In the earliest stages, as the children counted, I checked for one-to-one correspondence and a knowledge of the sequence of counting numbers. At later stages, I noted what counting strategies the children used. Did they count in ones, twos, and so on? Did they put aside each cube (or mark each circle) as they counted? Did they arrange the cubes in patterns? Did they group in tens and hundreds?

Another counting task set was to arrange a number of cubes in such a way that anyone could see how many there were without needing to count. I noted whether the children grouped the cubes in easily recognised patterns.

Problem-solving strategies

When I gave the children a problem I noted the strategies they used to solve it. Did they focus on the task? Did they work systematically and logically? Were they successful in solving the problem? Sometimes I suggested they check their answer by using a different strategy.

One problem I set was this one.

On a farm there was a snake in the grass. It saw twenty-two legs in the sheep yard. How many sheep did it see?

Most children drew a picture to work out this problem; some took a long time, drawing sheep complete with facial features and wool, while others quickly drew lines or dots to represent the legs, circling four at a time (or two at a time if they did not focus appropriately on the problem). Some children didn't know what to do about the two spare legs; others worked out solutions such as a farmer being in the yard with the sheep, or one sheep being half in and half out of the yard. A few children raised the possibility that some of the legs belonged to a sheep dog or a straying cow.

Concrete calculations

The children were given problems which required them to add, subtract, multiply and divide. I supplied them with a range of concrete materials to use in working out the answer, plus pencils and paper. This made it possible to note which materials the children chose to use and the ways in which they used them. I also noted when the children started to prefer using pencil and paper for calculations, either for visual representations of numbers or for the conventional number symbols.

Pencil-and-paper calculations

To provide a continuous record of their development I sometimes asked the children to do number calculations on a page in the exercise book in which I kept their records.

It was then possible to note and date when and how each child used visual representations of numbers and written number symbols.

Mental calculations

Sometimes I posed a problem requiring number calculation and provided neither concrete materials nor pencil and paper: the children had to work out the answer in their heads. I asked them to explain how they were going about finding the answer, and noted the strategies the children used to add, multiply, divide and find differences.

Investigations

Some problems requiring investigation were set. During a maths chat I posed a question such as "What can children do in three seconds?" and asked the child to explain how he or she would do the investigation. I noted whether the child formed a hypothesis and made an appropriate plan of action.

The child then carried out the investigation independently. I checked on progress throughout the investigation, noting whether the work was proceeding logically. At the end, we discussed what discoveries had been made. I also asked whether the child had thought of any further questions during the investigation.

Observing children working

As the children worked on mathematics I entered brief observations in a notebook that was always at hand and later copied them into the children's record books.

I noted such things as:

- each child's ability to work independently, cooperatively, creatively and competently,
- how they solved problems (comparing notes over several weeks to check they were each using a range of strategies),
- whether they worked logically and systematically,
- what stage of problem writing each child had reached, and
- how they worked through their own problems as they wrote them (did they use concrete, visual or abstract models of numbers?).

As the children solved each other's problems, I noted each child's level of involvement. Were they enthusiastic in their responses? How quick were they? How often did they raise their hand to make a contribution? Did they sit back and let the others offer ideas? Did they offer new ideas or did they mostly pick up the ideas of others? What stage in their computations had they reached (see p.50)?

I noted whether the children started by looking for patterns as they worked on number investigations. Were they continually extending their repertoire of patterns? Were they focusing on addition, subtraction, multiplication and division?

The children's problems

It probably would have been a good idea to have kept each child's written problems in a container (such as a shoebox). This would have provided a concrete record of their work. Instead, the children took their problem books home after they shared them with the class. (Several children stored their problems in shoeboxes at home.)

I kept a checklist of the number and types of problems each child wrote and the stages they were progressing through. I marked off the checklist as the children shared their problems.

I also checked whether all the children were writing problems regularly and progressing through the stages.

Program evaluation

The effectiveness of the program was continually evaluated by considering three basic questions:

- Was the aim appropriate?
- Was the planned program content consistent with the aim?
- Was the children's work consistent with the aim?

Was the aim appropriate?

The aim of the program was to develop in children the ability to creatively and competently pose and solve a range of problems and investigate a range of mathematical topics.

At the beginning of Year One, I organised a meeting of the children's parents to discuss the year's program. Two thirds of the children had one or both parents at the meeting. We discussed the parents' expectations, their values regarding mathematics, and the aims of the program. I described the types of activities the children would be engaged in and explained how these related to the aim.

At the outset of the meeting the parents said they expected and wanted their children to do regular written exercises. After discussion of those aspects of mathematics the parents considered important, they realised that regular written exercises were not as necessary as they had thought. By the end of the meeting, the parents were very enthusiastic about the program and were not at all concerned that their children would not be taking home exercise books full of written computations.

Throughout the program the parents offered strong support for what I was doing and often commented favourably on the children's progress in mathematics.

Was the planned program content consistent with the aim?

To meet the objectives of the school's mathematics curriculum, I had to ensure continually that the children were developing certain concepts and skills in the areas of number, measurement, space and logic.

The children spontaneously met most of the objectives as they posed and solved problems, and carried out investigations.

Activities had to be planned to cover the objectives the children were not meeting. When I planned such an activity I checked that it was consistent with the program aim. All topics were set in the form of problems and investigations which allowed the children to work creatively.

Was the children's work consistent with the aim of the program?

As the program was concerned with the children taking responsibility for generating much of the work, the ratio of child-initiated work to teacher-initiated work was important. I recorded the development of the children's ability to pose and solve problems and their increasing range of investigation skills.

The children's ability to think creatively and independently was monitored. Their range of responses to any one topic and the range of responses from each child over time indicated that the children were able to do so.

I set further open-ended tasks whenever misconceptions arose. It was tempting sometimes to step in and demonstrate the correct way to solve a problem or make a calculation. But this would have conflicted with the program's aim and probably would not have helped the child's understanding. It would simply have given the child a technique to follow.

Involving the children in evaluation

I involved the children in evaluation as much as possible.

Sometimes I asked them how the problems they were writing were different from those they had written previously. In this way they were able to reflect on their own progress in generating problems. They needed help to analyse the various types of problems they wrote. We discussed the significance of producing a variety of problems and related their problems to the range of "real world" problems.

We also discussed the increasing range of problem-solving strategies the children were developing. Were they each using a variety of strategies? Why did they need to be able to use several strategies? What did they do if a strategy was not successful? Did they enjoy working with numbers? What did they use to do calculations? Did they try different calculation strategies? What did they learn as they discussed each other's strategies?

The children were asked why they thought we did investigations. Were they learning new ways to do investigations? What were they learning as they did investigations? Were number investigations important? What did they learn as they investigated numbers?

We considered their measurement skills and concepts. Were they sure how to use devices such as rulers and tape measures, scales and measuring jugs? Did they confidently use clocks and stopwatches? Were the children helped by their experiences with measuring devices to estimate measurements fairly accurately? Was it important to be able to estimate?

The development of the children's spatial concepts was also examined. Was it important to learn about lines, angles and shapes? Did the children see any relationships between the various regular shapes? Did their knowledge of some shapes help them find out about other shapes? Were they discovering useful ways to draw and construct regular shapes?

Together we assessed the effectiveness of the games we made. Was each game serving its purpose? What were the children learning as they played the games? What were the most popular games and why? Did any games need changing?

POSING PROBLEMS

P R O B L E M S

2

2.1 Making a start with problems

Presenting problems

I chose to present many of the early problems in book form as the children were enthusiastic about reading and I wanted to integrate mathematics into the language program. I made several books for the children to read, each book containing a problem. The problems were written as very short stories accompanied by illustrations. There was usually one sentence to a page. The books had pages of sturdy, coloured cardboard held together with spiral binding.

I did not present the problems in any particular sequence, nor were the problems at any one time confined to one type. It is important to present a range of problem types at any one time so that children are encouraged to carefully attend to each problem.

Addition problems

Some of the problems were simple one- or two-step addition problems.

TEDDIES IN THE PARK

Three teddies were in the park. (One red teddy, one green teddy and one yellow teddy are pictured.) Two more teddies came with a ball. (One blue teddy and one orange teddy are pictured.) All the teddies played with the ball. How many teddies were playing?

Multiplication problems

Some of the problems involve multiplication, which for children at this stage was performed by repeated addition.

FRED'S FLEAS

Here is Fred. He has four itchy legs. On each leg there are three fleas. How many fleas are on Fred?

Subtraction problems

I presented three kinds of subtraction problems. One focused on finding the difference between two quantities.

CHERRIES

Adam has seven cherries. Karen has four cherries. How many more cherries does Adam have?

Another type of subtraction problem involved adding on to one quantity to find how many more were needed or how many had been removed.

EGGS

Dad needed six eggs to make a cake. He found four eggs in the fridge. How many more eggs did Dad need?

THE BOX OF CHOCOLATES

I had a box of chocolates. There were ten chocolates in the box. My little sister sneaked into my room and ate some of my chocolates. When I looked in the box again there were only seven left. How many chocolates had my naughty sister eaten?

The third type of subtraction involved taking away one quantity from another.

PATTY CAKES

There were eight chocolate patty cakes on a plate. Stacey ate two of them. How many cakes were left on the plate?

Division problems

There were two types of division problems. In problems of partition division, the total quantity and the number of shares were given. The children had to find the size of each share.

STRAWBERRIES

There are twelve strawberries on a plate. Sam wants some. Liza wants some. John wants some. If they share them fairly, how many strawberries can each one have?

LITTLE CAT

Fat Cat ate six mice. Little Cat ate half as many. How many mice did Little Cat eat?

Craig later wrote a problem about carrots based on the "Strawberries" problem.

In problems of quotition division, the total quantity and the size of each share were given. The children had to find the number of shares.

OMELETTES

Mum wanted to make some omelettes. She found ten eggs in the fridge. She needed two eggs for each omelette. How many omelettes could Mum make?

Combining operations

Some problems combined operations. The following example combines addition and subtraction.

GRANDPA'S SOUP

Grandpa made some soup. He put four tomatoes in the pot. He put two onions in the pot. He put three carrots in the pot. Grandma came in. "I don't like carrots very much," she said. So Grandpa took out two carrots. Mum came in. "I love tomatoes," she said. So Grandpa put another tomato in the pot. Dad came in. "I don't like too many onions," he said. So Grandpa took out one onion. How many vegetables did Grandpa put in the soup?

Puzzle problems

Some problems involved more than simply the application of one or more of the four basic operations. The children called these trickier problems "puzzle problems" and "big-brain-here-we-go-again problems".

The puzzle problems were generally adaptations of some found in published collections. I adapted them to suit the interests and levels of understanding of young children.

THE BIRTHDAY PARTY

Red Teddy's birthday was on Saturday. Green Teddy's birthday was on Saturday. Black Teddy's birthday was on Saturday. All on the same day! So they all had a party together. Just the three of them. How many presents were at the party?

RUNNING TEDDIES

Five teddies had a race. Red Teddy came first. Green Teddy came last. Orange Teddy was behind Blue Teddy. Yellow Teddy was after Orange Teddy. Which teddy came second?

I presented some problems as picture problems, without any words. These were based on visual patterns. The children had to work out what would be the next picture in any sequence.

MEASLES ARE VERY CATCHING

What happens next ?

How the children used the problem books

The books were available for the children to use at various times throughout the day. They could use them when they had finished set work, when it was time to play mathematics games, and at quiet reading time in the afternoon.

Unifix cubes (variously coloured interlocking plastic cubes) were available in the classroom and I planned that the children would use them to work out the problems. In the books, the relevant items in the problems were colour matched to Unifix cubes. For instance, in a problem about licorice, the children could use black cubes to represent the licorice. In the problem *Measles are very catching* (see above), the children used red cubes for the measle spots.

The children did not rely entirely on the Unifix cubes, sometimes acting out problems and sometimes drawing pictures to help find answers.

They returned many times to the various kinds of problem books, usually selecting a few of the books and a container of Unifix cubes. They enjoyed working in pairs on the problems. I encouraged them to work together as discussion about how to solve problems proved useful.

2.2 Helping the children begin to pose problems

Making up oral problems

The children helped me to make up oral problems. These were often based on my written problems or on themes we were working on.

For example, when we shared one problem I had written, *The hungry shark*, the children enthusiastically made up other problems about hungry sharks. The children found in a book some information about what sharks eat and they used this to help them with their problems.

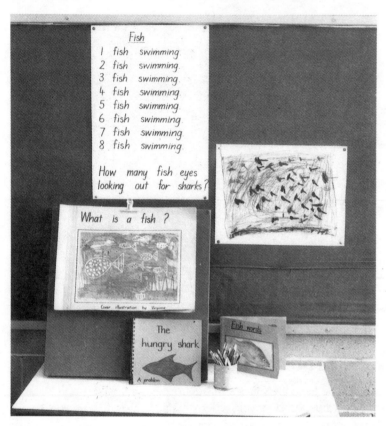

When we studied flies and sang the song about flies in the buttermilk, the children suggested a range of other foods flies might like, and made up related problems.

Five flies in the buttermilk, shoo, shoo, shoo. Three flies in the honey, shoo, shoo, shoo. Two flies in the strawberry jam, shoo, shoo, shoo. How many flies to shoo, shoo, shoo?

Sometimes the children shared their "news" and we found these items a source of problems. Here is one example.

Kate bought four bangles. Each one cost thirty cents. How much did Kate spend?

The children became increasingly alert to real problems. As I pegged up four paintings one day, Tim said, "I know a problem about that. How many pegs do you need for four paintings if you use two pegs for each painting?"

Shared writing of problems

I made some of the children's oral problems into books which the children illustrated. These books were very popular with the class and the children began suggesting which oral problems they wanted written down. Instead of saying, "Let's make up a problem", the children started asking, "Can we write a problem?"

Often something we were writing together was turned into a problem. When one of the children told us that the class pet, a rabbit named Fluffy, had nearly bitten off her finger, I suggested we write about the incident together. On paper clipped to a nearby easel I wrote:

Stacey patted Fluffy on his nose. Fluffy thought Stacey's finger was a carrot.

"And he bit it off," volunteered one child. (Exaggeration was an accepted aspect of story writing!) Another child said, "We can make it a problem." So we did.

And he bit it off. How many fingers does Stacey have now?

Sometimes a story we had read was the source of a problem. After reading a book which listed several things a crocodile had eaten for lunch, we wrote the following problem.

CROCODILE'S LUNCH

Crocodile wasn't very hungry. He ate 4 egg and tomato sandwiches. He ate 8 pieces of bread and butter. He ate 2 chocolate biscuits. He ate 2 pieces of fruit cake. How many things did Crocodile eat?

Children starting to write problems

Within a few weeks of the introduction of the problem books, some children spontaneously began writing problems. Ready-made blank books were always at hand in the classroom. When the rest of the children saw their classmates writing problems, they all started to do so.

The first books the children wrote were closely modelled on the ones I had written. For instance, I wrote *The fruit bowl* then Terri produced a similar one about vegetables.

THE FRUIT BOWL

In the fruit bowl were ... 3 apples ... and an orange ... and a banana. I ate 2 apples. How many pieces of fruit were left in the bowl?

THE VEGETABLE BOWL

In the bowl were ... 5 beans ... and 4 radishes ... and a carrot. I ate 3 radishes. How many pieces of vegetable were left in the bowl?

When Terri showed me her book, she eagerly watched as I read it, worked out the answer, and wrote, "Were there seven vegetables left in the bowl?" Terri took the book away, checked the answer using Unifix cubes and wrote, "Yes".

Terri had written her problem by following the story line in *The fruit bowl*, changing the fruit to vegetables, and changing the numbers. She had made no use of concrete materials such as Unifix cubes as she wrote. Craig used the same method to write a problem based on the book *Strawberries*, described previously.

CARROTS

There are 10 carrots on a plate. Hayley wants some. Tim wants some. Mrs Skinner wants some. How many carrots can each one have?

Craig showed me his book and I asked him to work out the answer with me. He asked Tim, Hayley and me to stand around a table on which he put a plate holding ten orange Unifix cubes. We each took one "carrot" at a time until we were holding three each and there was one remaining on the plate. Craig looked down at the one on the plate, looked at our hands to see how many we were holding, and paused momentarily. He turned to what he had written, crossed off the "ten" and wrote "nine" in its place.

Craig later shared his problem with the class and explained why he had made the change. The children discussed the importance of working out their own problems so that they made sense. They decided it would be a good idea to use the Unifix cubes when they were writing problems.

Within days, one of the children wrote the answer at the end of his problem and covered it with a lift-up flap. The other children liked this idea and everyone soon started doing the same.

The children continued writing problems for the rest of the Kindergarten year. Gradually they became less dependent upon the starter problems and many of the children began writing original problems, like these two.

SANTA IS COMING

Here is a Christmas tree. These are the decorations. These are the presents. 3 of mine. 2 of Dad's. 1 of Mum's. How many presents?

SAhtAis coming
hire is A xmAs
tnee
these Are the
DeCK rAsh's
these Are the prisints
three of mine
two of DADS
one of mums
how meny prisnts

In the city there were 4 Christmas trees. Every tree had 20 lights. How many lights were in the city?

Setting up a problem-writing area

During the first term of Year One the children were showing such an interest in writing problem books that I set up one area of the room for all the materials essential to compiling them. The children used the area in the morning language sessions.

The area contained a table with eight chairs, and the following materials for producing the books:

- Blank books of six pages each, made from recycled computer paper, and measuring about 18 cm x 13 cm
- A stapler, to join books together if problems needed more than six pages
- A date stamp, to date the books
- Pencils, crayons, and felt-tip pens
- Scrap paper, for trying out ideas
- Coloured paper squares, to be used as flaps for covering answers
- Scissors, because the children sometimes cut the coloured paper squares into other shapes
- Sticky tape
- Plastic replica coins, coin stamps and stamp-pad
- Unifix cubes
- MAB blocks (wooden blocks based on a unit measurement of one cubic centimetre). We used single blocks ("ones"), and long blocks comprised of ten units ("tens"). Later, "hundreds" were also used.
- A container labelled "Problems for sharing", into which the children put their completed books.

The children began making a problem book by writing the title on the cover. I found it useful to check the spelling of the title at that stage, because the words in the title usually appeared several times in the book. The children then continued independently. There was always much chatter at the table, mostly about the work in hand, as the children showed a helpful interest in each other's work.

Sharing the children's problems

The children shared all their writing in some way. Some was shared orally: that is, the children read it to the class or to a group of friends. We made good copies of some pieces of writing and these were put into the class library.

The children's problems were shared in the same way. When the children read out their problems, the other children worked out the answers. How this was done will be discussed in a later section. (See p.42.)

2.3 Monitoring the children's progress with posing problems

The children's problem writing developed through eight major stages. Most of the problems arose spontaneously and the children progressed through the stages without my direction. They influenced each other to the extent that when a child or group of children embarked on a new stage, most of the others followed their example within days.

The stages described here are those which developed from my program. They may not be the same as those which will occur in other classrooms where children's interests and ability will be different and problems will vary. However, they serve as a guide to what might develop in other classrooms, and indicate aspects to look for.

Each child worked with the numbers and concepts with which he or she was confident. The benefits of this were twofold. First, the children were not failing at mathematics. Each was working at his or her own level of understanding. They were not being asked to do things of which they had no understanding. Second, I was able to assess each child's progress in terms of what he or she was confident to do.

Stage one: Copying problems

The first stage of writing problems was characterised by copying ideas and problem structures. At this stage the children generally based their problems on ones I had written. Most of the children passed through this stage in Kindergarten or early Year One. Children who joined the class at a later time began at this first, copying stage, but instead of modelling their books on mine they usually modelled them on the ones the other children were producing at the time.

Yvonne, who came into the class towards the end of Year One, spoke very little English and had had very little school experience. She spent her first day in the classroom watching all that was going on. On the second day she went immediately to the problem writing table, picked up a blank book, and drew a rabbit on the cover. She asked me to write "rabbit". Her book followed a number sequence that a few children had used in their books on the previous day.

RABBITS

---

1 rabbit. 2 rabbits. 3 rabbits. 4 rabbits. 5 rabbits. How many rabbits?

On the following days she wrote similar books about things like houses, cats, dogs, and flowers. This was the only writing she was confident to do for her first three weeks in the class. For this child, problem writing gave purpose not only to mathematics but to writing.

Jackie entered the program in the middle of Year Two and began her problem writing by copying the sort of problems the other children were writing. The children were mostly working with numbers in the thousands and many of the problems dealt with money. This was Jackie's first problem.

THE ROBBER

The bank had $5000. A robber stole $5. How much money was left in the bank?

Her answer was $000. Clearly, copying the other children was not successful for this girl, so I worked with her through some of the problem books I had written. She very soon began working with numbers and problem structures with which she was confident.

Stage two: Addition or subtraction problems

During the second stage the children began to write original problems. These problems usually featured either addition or subtraction. All three types of subtraction (finding differences, amending deficiencies, taking away) were represented. Only very occasionally at this stage did children write division or multiplication problems. The following problem is typical.

> **Textas**
>
> I had ten textas.
> Alison left 3 lids off my textas and ruined them.
> Mitchell took 1 of my textas.
> I bit him.
> How many textas did I have?

After the children had moved on to the third stage, they didn't leave stage two entirely. When they began using numbers beyond twenty, and later when they began using numbers beyond one hundred, many children reverted to writing second stage addition or subtraction problems.

MUDDY FOOTPRINTS

100 muddy footprints on the kitchen floor …
10 muddy footprints through the door …
20 muddy footprints on my bed …
30 muddy footprints on my head …
How many footprints did my cat leave?

> Mr Moore had 694 dogs. Mrs Skinner had 628 dogs. How many more dogs did Mr Moore have?

> **Money**
>
> Erica had one dollar.
> Terri had one dollar
> Sarah had one dollar too...
> and Jenny had 50c.
> How many cents does Jenny need to make one dollar? How much money do they all have together?

Stage three: "Came and went" problems

Each of the problems written during the third stage combined addition and subtraction, and the children labelled them "came and went" problems. This stage lasted from about the middle of Year One to early Year Two. During this time there was a gradual increase in the size of the numbers the children were working with.

CATS

18 cats. 10 cats more. 7 dogs ran and chased the cats. 7 cats go. 20 cats see cat food and go away to eat it all. 40 cats come and 20 cats more. 1 goes. 2 go. 8 cats go and 4 cats come back. 20 cats go on motorcycles. 6 come back. How many cats?

SPIKE MILLIGAN LOSES HIS HAIR

Spike had 400 bits of hair. He lost 300 bits of hair. He lost 50 more when a baby tore them out. He cried so much that he lost 10 more. He watered them. 100 more grew. He got mad and tore out 50 more. How many left?

> Money
>
> If I had $3·50   and Karen
> gave me $10·75   and I lost
> 25 cents   and found 50c
> how much money   do I have?

Stage four: Multiplication or division problems

Stage four problems involved either multiplication or division.

HOT CHIPS

Adam and Andrew had hot chips. There were 20 in the container. How many hot chips could they have each?

The answer to the above problem was ten. When the problem was shared with the class, the children overlooked the fact that the problem did not state that the chips had to be evenly distributed between the two boys. With this type of problem, the children always assumed that the writer intended an even distribution of the objects.

LEGS

10 cows. How many legs?

24 legs. How many dogs?

60 legs. How many birds?

78 cats. How many legs?

24 tentacles. How many octopuses?

PEPPER GRAINS

Perceptor looked at 25 pepper grains and he forgot to focus on it so it looked like it was 3 times as much. How many pepper grains did he see?

GARFIELD

Garfield kicked and punched Odie lots of times and Odie got so vicious that he kicked and punched as well. All Garfield's kicks and punches equalled 66 all together and there were the same of each. Odie's were like that too except it was 72. How many punches did Odie get from Garfield? And how many kicks did Odie get from Garfield? And how many punches did Garfield get from Odie? And how many kicks did Garfield get from Odie?

The children used calculators to write some multiplication and division problems. It was interesting to note that every time they used calculators the problems they wrote involved much larger numbers than they ordinarily used.

A HORSE FARM

6789 horses. How many tails?

8956 horses. How many ears?

10 967 horses. How many legs?

8000 horses. How many eyes?

MONEY

There was $5224 worth of toys and 4 men had to split it up. How much money was each man's share worth?

Stage five: Combining any of the four operations in problems

Stage five problems combined multiplication, division, addition and subtraction.

DINOSAURS

8 dinosaurs had 4 lollipops each and they wanted to share with some other dinosaurs so that they could all have one of the lollipops each. How many more dinosaurs had to come?

The knock on the door
Lisa
Lisa made 626 choclets.
Then ,knock 'knock' Jennifer
was at the door. And Lisa
said " do you want to share

my choclets." "Yes please" said
Jennifer. Now we get?   313
Then   -Knock- Knock-
Mrs skinner and Mr Moore
were at the door. "Come
in" said Jennifer. Would you
like to share our choclets.
Yes please said Mrs skinner and
Mr Moore. Now we get? 156½

Then   -Knock- -knock- Mr Amos
and   Mrs Osborn and
Mrs Pawle and Mr Dowd
were at the door. "come in"
said Lisa " do you want to
share our choclets" said Lisa.
"yes please" they said.
now we get?   78¢

Often children wrote problems which seemed like simple addition problems
until the last line. These problems ended with a question which set the reader
the task of doubling or quadrupling what had gone before.

SUNGLASSES

**67 girls wearing sunglasses. Another 87 girls wearing sunglasses. How
many lenses?**

Nostrils Smelling

1 nose smelling dirty
Socks.

2   noses smelling dirty socks.

3   noses   smelling dirty socks.

4   noses smelling dirty socks

How many   nostrils
smelling dirty Socks ?

Stage six: Series of problems

Stage six was characterised by books containing several problems rather than just one, and most of the books featured a mixture of addition, multiplication, subtraction and division problems. Children sometimes worked in pairs on these books.

When Lisa wrote at the end of a book, "How many in the whole book?", every other child copied her idea.

PROBLEM BABIES

O nce there were 6 babies. They solved problems for themselves. Once they bought 100 pieces of gum. If they had 9 pieces each, how many would be left over?

Once there were 40 babies. They wet their nappies 6 times a day. And the first baby always wet her nappy two more times. How many wet nappies in a day?

Once there were 10 babies and Mum said "Time for a bath", but only 2 went to the bath. So the others got 10 smacks each. How many smacks? Then they got in the bath and never got out.

How many babies in the whole book?

The 3 naughty girls
        by Karen

10 Smacks from the 3 naughty
girls 6 more 8 more
10 more   how many smacks?

        34

60 Smacks from 3 naughty girls.
33 missed.

        27

70 Smacks from 3 naughty girls.
7 missed.   63

how many smacks from
each naughty girl?

            21

How many Smacks all
together?

        124

Stage seven: Longer series of problems

In stage seven, problem writing became a more long-term task. It began when the book *Problem babies* (described above), grew into a series of books. Other children then worked in pairs or groups of up to six to produce a series of books on a theme. There were up to twenty books in a series. The children would work on their series for days or weeks, usually packaging them in a decorative box and often writing dedications, introductions and blurbs.

As with the books in stage six, a range of problem types was presented within a series. The children explored new possibilities for problems, including fractions, time, money and measurement. And almost all the series ended with the question, "How many in the whole series?" The following excerpt from one series demonstrates the range of problems the children devised.

GADGET

Gadget's clock said 8:25. The real time was 9:15. How slow was Gadget's clock?

Mad Cat ate 20 mice and 80 rats. Each mouse had a mass of 50g. Each rat had a mass of 80g. How many grams did Mad Cat eat?

There were 36 children in Penny's class. They each made 15 paper planes. How many planes all together?

Chief Quimby thought Gadget solved 100 crimes. Actually Penny solved three-quarters of them and Brain solved a tenth of them. So how many crimes did Gadget solve?

Gadget's arms spring out 60 times every 20 seconds. How long would it take for them to spring out 120 times? How many times would they spring out in 70 seconds?

Stage eight: Abstract number problems

In the final stage the children showed an interest in numbers abstracted from concrete settings. Until then, most problems had been encompassed in stories, however brief. The move to working with abstract numbers was a very important development. Formal mathematics, which deals with abstract numbers, is a powerful problem-solving tool. It enables simple problem-solving (e.g. requiring the application of a mathematical operation such as multiplication) to be done efficiently, with speed and accuracy; and it is fundamental to more complex problem-solving.

The first problems in this stage were vaguely linked with a concrete setting.

martians

$$
\begin{aligned}
&5+ \\
&5+ \\
&5+ \\
&5+ \\
&5+ \\
&5+ \\
&500+ \\
&100+ \\
&5 \\
&5+ \\
&5+ \\
&5+
\end{aligned}
\quad
\begin{aligned}
&5+ \\
&5+ \\
&5+ \\
&1000+ \\
&5+ \\
&5+ \\
&55+ \\
&50+ \\
&5+ \\
&5+ \\
&5+ \\
&5+
\end{aligned}
\quad
\begin{aligned}
&5+ \\
&5+ \\
&5+ \\
&5+ \\
&5+ \\
&5+ \\
&5+ \\
&5+ \\
&5+ \\
&55+ \\
&155+
\end{aligned}
\quad
\begin{aligned}
&5+ \\
&5+ \\
&5+ \\
&5+ \\
&5+ \\
&5+ \\
&5+ \\
&5+ \\
&100+ \\
&5+ \\
&5+ \\
&5
\end{aligned}
$$

How many martians in vaded earth ?

ROBBER PIGS
BABIES
The robber pig had 5 babies and then ÷ by 5 then it x by 5 then it − 5 How many babies ?

Later problems were divorced entirely from concrete settings and were usually written as number sentences with one of the numbers or operation symbols covered with a lift-up flap. Craig and Damien made a set of four books which they titled, *Easy, Hard, Very hard* and *Impossible*. They wrote number problems in these in the form of number sentences. In the *Easy* book they put number sentences they had worked out in their heads; in the *Hard* book they wrote number sentences they had worked out on paper; in the *Very hard* book they wrote number sentences they had worked out on calculators. They were surprised that they had nothing to put in the *Impossible* book.

The children did not leave stage seven entirely while they wrote abstract number problems, but moved between the two final stages.

In the latter part of Year Two all the children were working with abstract numbers. I believe that one of the most crucial things a teacher can do in the early years of school is to help children move from informal, concrete mathematics to formal, abstract mathematics. In this program, the link between concrete and abstract numbers was made by the children themselves as they were given the freedom and motivation to develop at their own pace.

2.4 When progress did not occur

Children who did not progress

There was one child who rarely wrote problems. To overcome his consequent lack of progress in problem posing, I asked him to make up verbal problems during our maths chats and during class problem-solving sessions. He became interested in creating problems in this way and started to write problems. He never wrote as many as most of the others, but he did become quite successful at posing problems, and progressed through the same stages as the other children (as outlined in the previous section).

A few children were slow to move from one stage to another and I asked them, too, to make up verbal problems in the class problem sharing sessions. For instance, when Jenny had shared a written division problem, the children who hadn't started writing division problems were asked to "make up some problems like Jenny's". Sometimes small groups of children worked with me making up problems of a certain type.

Topics the children did not cover

Occasionally I initiated problem writing to introduce concepts the children rarely used in their own work. For example, the children did not initiate work on time/distance/rate problems. To introduce the concept, I set the research topic, "How fast can animals move?" The children timed some animals, such as snails, woodlice and silverfish. They looked up books to find the speed of other animals. Then I asked them to write some problems based on what they had found.

Our snail Blob goes 3 cm in one minute. How long will it take him to go 12 cm?

Fraction problems

Only a few children used fractions in their problems. Because they weren't dealt with very often and because the school curriculum dictated that they had to be introduced in Year Two, I set fraction topics for investigation. The children almost always worked with shapes rather than with numbers. I linked the two aspects by suggesting topics such as "Cherry pie", in which the children divided round pies easily into halves, quarters and eighths. Dividing them into other fractions such as thirds was more difficult, but the children successfully explored such possibilities. Once they had divided a pie into a number of equal parts, they found they had a basis for dividing the cherries: they distributed them equally among the slices of pie.

To follow up these investigations and to introduce fractions into children's problem writing, we had group problem writing to focus on fractions. One topic was blackbird pies, based on the traditional children's rhyme, "Sing a Song of Sixpence". Here is one group's problem.

BLACKBIRD PIE

Once upon a time there was a queen, a king, a prince and a princess. They had a pie with 24 blackbirds in it. If they had a quarter of the pie each, how many blackbirds would they each get? But the king and queen decided it wasn't fair because they were much bigger than the prince and princess. So they decided to have twice as much as the children. How many blackbirds did everybody get?

Posing puzzle problems

The children rarely wrote original puzzle problems. The following one was written at Christmas time at the end of Year One.

SANTA'S FLAT

Natasha lives in a flat with a big number. All the flats are 1, 2, 3, 4, 5, 6, 7, 8, 9 and 10. Santa lives in one of the flats too. Which one does he live in? It's an even number. It's not a square number. It's not a triangular number. It's next door to Natasha.

When this problem was written, other children tried writing similar problems.

What number is my house?

It is an odd number.

It is in the $3\frac{1}{2}$s pattern.

It is less than $10\frac{1}{2}$ more than $3\frac{1}{2}$.

The children sometimes spontaneously wrote their own versions of puzzle problems I presented. The following problem is based on *Running teddies* (discussed on p.25).

THE DINO RACE

Six dinosaurs had a race. Two dinosaurs tied for second. Brachiosaurus was one of them. Little D was two places ahead of Ankylosaurus. Ankylosaurus beat Tyro! Diplodo was sleepy and came last! Stego was beaten by only one other dinosaur. Who won the race?

Again, some children wrote similar problems to *The dino race*. For those children who thought it was too difficult to write such problems, I led group sessions in which they worked together.

In class sessions we copied various types of puzzle problems. The children liked working in pairs to write some too.

PROBLEMS

[S]OLVING

3

3.1 Organising problem-solving

Whole-class problem-solving

In Years One and Two I led daily sessions in which the children worked together to solve each other's problems. We sat in a circle on the floor with problem-solving materials.

Initially the concrete materials we used were Unifix cubes, but once the children were familiar with MAB blocks they became the preferred materials. Pencil-and-paper calculations were popular in the latter half of Year Two. Each child always used those materials with which he or she was confident.

Each child who had written a problem on a given day would read out the problem, or ask me to do so. A pause after reading each page allowed the appropriate action to be carried out with the materials in the centre of our circle.

After a problem had been worked out, I signed the back of the book and usually returned it to the child who had written it. Some of the books were kept for use at other times. For example, I put aside several division problems for a time when we would be discussing division and relating formal division symbolism to problems (see p.120).

Small-group problem-solving

Having the children work in pairs on "puzzle problems" best ensured that they were all contributing ideas. Sometimes the children worked in groups of four to further develop cooperative problem-solving. Occasionally the children presented their own problems to small groups instead of to the whole class.

3.2 Developing problem-solving strategies

Approaching a problem

The children devised general strategies for tackling problems. They acted out some problems, made models of some, and drew pictures and diagrams to help work out others.

Acting out problems
When the children worked in pairs on the problem books they often looked for those featuring two characters so they could act out the problem.

Using models
When children used Unifix cubes to work out each other's problems they were often using the cubes not only to help them count but were also setting up a model of the problem. This was particularly evident when they were careful to match the colour of the Unifix cubes to the colour of the objects they were representing.

Drawing pictures

Sometimes children used drawings to help them work out simple problems such as the following, written by Trevor in Year Two.

CROCODILE EGGS

10 crocodiles went down to the river. 5 of them laid eggs. They laid 6 eggs each. A goanna ate 12 of the eggs. How many eggs were left?

The children who did drawings to work out this problem drew ten crocodiles by a river. They drew six eggs beside each of five crocodiles, crossed off or drew teeth marks in twelve eggs and counted the ones remaining.

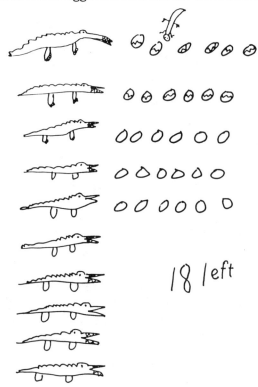

Drawing diagrams

When we were organising a concert item, we needed to arrange the children so that half were sitting and half were standing. The children began discussing ways to divide the class. Noting the children's interest in the discussion, I asked them to "use pencil and paper" to show how it could be done. I specifically avoided use of the word "drawing". Several children drew pictures or wrote a description of how it could be done. Two children drew diagrams. When the class shared the strategies they had used, the two diagrams attracted the most positive response from the other children.

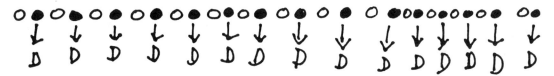

Karen's diagram

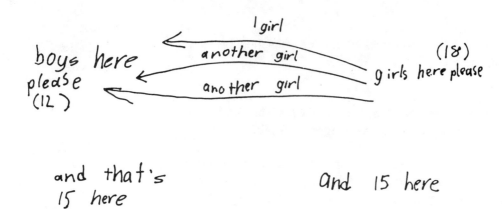

and that's
15 here

and 15 here

Timothy's diagram

Different strategies at work

All four of the above strategies – acting, making models, drawing pictures and drawing diagrams – were used to solve the following problem.

If four people gave each other a Christmas card, how many cards would there be?

Two groups of children acted out the problem, one group using books to represent the cards, the other group using pencils.

One group made a model, standing four MAB "tens" on end to represent the people in the problem and MAB "ones" to represent the cards.

One group drew a picture of four people, each one holding three cards addressed to the others.

One group drew a diagram, representing each person by a differently coloured dot. They distributed "cards" by drawing lines which matched the colour of the "person" giving the card. As they made a mark for each card they said, "He gives the others a card but he doesn't give himself one".

Karen said to her group, "It's just four threes. What's four threes? Twelve". She explained her answer by saying that there were four people and each person was given three cards. The group accepted her explanation.

David's group similarly accepted his explanation that, "They have to buy three cards each so it's twelve".

Distinguishing relevant information

An important problem-solving strategy is to distinguish between relevant and irrelevant information in a problem. The children quite often wrote problems featuring "tricks", as they liked to call them.

CRABS

I had 32 crabs. I caught 19 more. One more caught me on my toe and I grabbed it too. I saw 50 more. How many crabs did I have then?

The children finding the answer had to note that the fifty crabs which were merely seen were not to be counted amongst the caught crabs.

I had 20 cats, 2 tigers, 3 dogs, 24 lions and 17 fish. How many cats did I have?

In setting this problem, the writer's intention was that the tigers and lions be classified as cats. In fact the children working on it decided there were two answers, because the question was ambiguous. If only domestic cats were to be counted, the writer had twenty cats. If all cats were to be included, then there were forty-six cats. The children had to read the question carefully because there were extra animals included in the problem to distract them. A careless reader may have thought the task was to count all the animals mentioned.

The children learned to expect "tricks", so they paid careful attention to the language and sense of each problem.

Working systematically

The children came to realise the importance of working systematically through a problem. One child explained the process as, "You find a beginning and go till you find the end."

In a discussion on the value of working systematically, the children made the following comments:

- "You don't miss anything out."
- "You don't get frustrated."
- "It doesn't get complicated."
- "You don't mess it up."
- "If you get disturbed you can go back to where you were."
- "It's easy."

One of the earliest problems which gave rise to systematic work was to count the squares in the following picture.

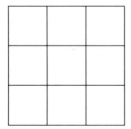

Some children noticed only the smallest squares so thought the answer was nine; some also noticed the largest square, so found ten squares; some children found one or more of the middle-sized squares; and some found all fourteen. The children who found all the squares worked systematically and later explained their methods to the class. One boy explained his method this way: "First I found all the one-ers and that was nine. Then I saw the three-er and I wondered if there were any two-ers so I looked and found four two-ers." (A "two-er" was a two-by-two arrangement.)

Simplifying problems

We made a model of an island and placed three towns — Unitown, Bitown and Tritown — along the island's only road. It was decided that the distance between Bitown and Tritown was twice the distance between Unitown and Bitown. I asked the children to work out how far it was between Bitown and Tritown if the road's total length was fifty-four kilometres.

One group working on the problem said, "It's too hard. Can we make the road shorter?"

At my suggestion, they then pretended that the road was nine kilometres long. They drew two roads on a piece of paper, a short road and a long road. After some discussion about what to do next, they distributed nine Unifix cubes in a 1:2 ratio onto the two roads. I asked them to explain to me how they had worked out the problem and then suggested they try the original problem. They found it easy to do by following the method they had devised for the shorter distance. Later they explained to the class the procedure of trying a simpler version of a problem before a more difficult version.

Tim suggested, "That's like when we were in Kindergarten and we wrote problems with very small numbers and now we use big numbers. You sort of get practice."

Relating problems

As their problem-solving skills developed, the children began to relate new problems to ones they had worked on already.

One problem was based on the traditional children's story "The Three Billy Goats Gruff". The children were asked to work out in how many ways the goats could cross the bridge if they went across one by one. Only those children who worked systematically found the six ways the goats could cross the bridge. No child worked systematically from the outset, but several devised systematic procedures as they progressed. As always, we had a follow-up demonstration and discussion of successful and unsuccessful methods of tackling the problem.

A later problem was to draw as many boats as possible using three elements (a hull, a mast and a sail) and three colours. A condition was that each of the elements had to be a different colour. Thus a boat could not have a yellow hull, a yellow mast and a yellow sail. As the children worked on the problem, some of them recognised the similarity between this problem and the goats one. "There'll be six boats", several children claimed with great excitement. Some children later extended this problem by withdrawing the condition that each of the elements had to be a different colour. This time, they were able to draw twenty-seven boats.

Several weeks after the Billy Goats Gruff problem, I suggested we write a similar one based on the children's story *The Enormous Turnip* (Ladybird Books, 1980). Working systematically, the children found all the possible arrangements of an old man, an old woman, a little boy and a little girl as they tried to pull up a turnip.

We then wrote the following story as a problem to present to another class. Every arrangement of the four people was pictured except one, and the task for the other class was to find which arrangement was missing.

Once there was a huge turnip growing in a garden. It was too big for Grandpa to pull up. It was too big for Grandpa and Grandma together to pull up. So they called their two grandchildren to come and help.

The girl pulled the boy, the boy pulled Grandma and Grandma pulled Grandpa. But the turnip did not come up.

"I know," said the girl, "I'll swap places with my brother." But still they could not pull up the turnip.

"I know," said the boy, "I'll go behind Grandpa." But the turnip wouldn't budge.

"I know," said Grandma, "I'll go to the back." But that didn't work either.

"Let me go behind Grandpa," said the girl. But still the turnip stayed in the ground.

"I'll go to the back again," said Grandma. And she did. But the turnip wouldn't move.

"Maybe I should go to the *front*," said Grandma. The turnip seemed to move just a little, but it didn't come up. They tried some other arrangements with Grandma at the front.

"Could I please have a turn at the front?" asked the boy. They tried some arrangements with the boy at the front. The turnip moved a little more.

"I'm tired," said Grandpa. "Let's go out to get a pizza instead."

"No," said the girl. "I haven't had a turn at the front yet." So they tried a few more times. At last the turnip came up!

"About time!" they all cried. "We only had one more arrangement to go!"

Finding patterns

Sometimes I set a series of related problems. A child suggested the following sequence after I presented the first problem.

HANDSHAKES

If there were three people at a party and they all shook hands with each other, how many handshakes would there be?

If there were four people, how many handshakes would there be?
If there were five people, how many handshakes would there be?
If there were six people, how many handshakes would there be?

The children, working in groups, used various strategies to work out these problems.

Some groups acted out the problems, working systematically so they would not miscount the handshakes. One group drew a picture for the first problem but found it difficult to do so for the following ones. Some groups drew diagrams, representing each person by a hand or an arbitrary mark and drawing lines between them to represent the handshakes. Several children became very interested in the patterns produced by their diagrams.

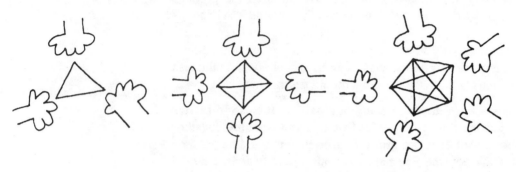

Most groups recorded their findings to the *Handshakes* problems in a rough table format and found interesting patterns amongst the numbers. Some children were able to extrapolate from the information in their tables to find how many handshakes there would be amongst larger numbers of people.

The children devised the following problems related to the *Handshakes* problems.

If three people were at a party and gave each other presents, how many presents would there be?
If the three people were French and gave each other two kisses, one on each cheek, how many kisses would there be?

The same questions were asked about four people, five people, and so on. The children found more interesting patterns when their findings were tabulated.

3.3 The teacher's role in problem-solving sessions

The children made the important problem-solving decisions. My role as a teacher was to organise the problem-solving sessions, find starter problems for the children to work on, and encourage follow-up discussions of strategies.

As the children work on problems

Once certain strategies had been discussed and tried out, it was helpful sometimes to suggest their use when groups were encountering difficulties. I would ask questions like:

- "Could you draw a diagram?"
- "Can you find a beginning and then work it out in some order?"
- "Why don't you draw a picture and put in all the things you know so far about the problem?"
- "Could you use a piece of paper for the river? Find something that you could use as a boat."

The development of each child was also monitored. As the children worked independently or in groups, I observed what they did and made notes to keep in my anecdotal records of each child's progress.

Guiding follow-up discussions

After a group problem-solving session the class always gathered to discuss what had been done. The focus of each discussion was on the progress the children had gone through to solve a problem. What did they do first? Why? If their first attempt was not successful what did they do next? Were they sure they had an appropriate answer? How many different ways did the children find to solve the problem? Which ways seemed to be the best? Why?

Even simple problems were discussed in this way. What are the best materials to use to solve this problem? Why? How will we use the materials to find the answer? Is that the only way? Would we use the same method for a similar problem with larger numbers?

3.4 The interrelationship of problem-solving and problem posing

Editing each other's work

The problem-solving sessions provided feedback to the problem writers as the children spontaneously edited each other's problems. They gave advice to each other on the use of appropriate language so the problems made sense and were unambiguous. The children learned to take more care with their problem writing and they sometimes rewrote their problems after a problem-solving session. Here are some examples.

EGGS

I needed 8 eggs and I had 6. Erin gave me 1. How many did I need?

When this problem was presented, Terri said, "You still need eight but you want us to say 'one' don't you? You should have said at the end, 'How many *more* eggs did I need?'"

Tom said, "She might be tricking us. She might be trying to get us to say 'one' and then she can say we're wrong."

Tom had 300 girlfriends. Half of them didn't resist. How many girlfriends did Tom have?

I wanted to know what Estelle meant by "resist"! "She means 'exist'," said Karen.

"I haven't even got one girlfriend," said Tom, "and no one would have three hundred." I reiterated the rule of not using classmates' names without their permission.

"It doesn't make sense," said Mitchell. "If someone has three hundred girlfriends but some of them don't exist then there can't be three hundred girlfriends."

"She should write, 'He *thought* he had three hundred girlfriends but half of them didn't exist'," suggested David.

MERRY'S PARTY

Merry had a birthday. She invited 11 people. Mummy bought 6 bags of lollies and chips. How many bags did each child get?

Brendan said, "It depends on how many brothers and sisters Merry has, because they would be at the party too."

"Did her mum buy six bags of lollies and six bags of chips or did she buy six all together?" asked Felicia.

Thea decided to take her book away and rewrite it. The second version of the problem follows.

Merry had a birthday. She didn't have any brothers or sisters. She invited 11 friends to her party. Mummy bought 6 bags of lollies and 6 bags of chips. How many bags of chips and how many bags of lollies did each child get?

Exchanging ideas

As new problem topics and structures appeared, the other children copied them and tried to improve on them. The children constantly tried to write more difficult problems to challenge each other. In this way, many new concepts were explored. For instance, when one child investigated fractions and started writing fraction problems involving unit fractions such as sixths, several other children became interested. Some of them wrote "harder" problems with unit fractions such as twentieths or sixtieths.

3.5 The development of computation skills through problem-solving

Problem-solving presented the children with the opportunity to develop computation skills in a purposeful context. I did not demonstrate any computation procedures; the children devised their own ways to add, subtract, multiply and divide when the need arose. Computation procedures were not ends in themselves in our classroom, but were tools for problem solving.

The children's computation skills developed spontaneously through six stages. They are described here as a suggested sequence that teachers could look for with any group of early primary children.

Stage one: Counting

During the earliest stage the children used concrete objects (usually Unifix cubes) to work out the problems. They added, subtracted, multiplied or divided and then counted the cubes to find an answer.

Stage two: Grouping and counting

The children began to group the Unifix cubes in tens as they were working out problems. Once they started to do this, I put together many of the Unifix cubes in tens and stored them in a plastic box. Each "ten" was made up of cubes of the one colour. A second container held single Unifix cubes which we called "ones".

If a problem involved removing some cubes from a "ten", the children simply pulled apart the cubes. After a while the children made a rule that no Unifix cubes would be joined unless a "ten" could be formed. This made it easier for the children to distinguish quickly how many "tens" they had and how many "ones". If any cubes had to be removed from a "ten", all the other cubes forming that "ten" had to be pulled apart as they would no longer form a "ten".

Stage three: Exchanging

Once the MAB blocks were introduced through games (see p.81) they soon became the preferred materials for problem-solving. The children found the MAB "tens", which were permanently joined, to be more convenient than the Unifix "tens" which sometimes fell apart or could mistakenly contain nine or eleven cubes. The use of MAB blocks led the children to develop the concept of exchanging.

When the MAB blocks were used, I would designate one child to be in charge of the container of "ones", another to be in charge of the "tens" and a third child to be in charge of the "hundreds" (once problems requiring the use of hundreds were being produced). During each session, the containers of blocks would change hands a few times.

The child with the container of "ones" was the only child who could put "ones" into the centre of the circle the children formed. The child with the "tens" was the only child to put out the "tens", and so on. Other children were chosen to operate on the blocks as the need arose.

An example of the process of solving a problem is illustrated in the following dialogue.

Tom was chosen to read his problem, *Sausages*. Jenny had the container of MAB "ones" and Alison had the container of "tens".

"There were nine sausages," read Tom.

Jenny put nine "ones" into the centre of the circle.

"Smash, bang, two were gone," continued Tom. Lots of hands went up.

"Stacey," I said. Stacey took two of the "ones" from the middle and returned them to Jenny's container.

Tom read, "They made six more".

Jenny put out six "ones". All hands shot up.

"Mitchell," I said. Mitchell picked up ten "ones", returned them to the "ones" container and called, "Ten". Alison put out a "ten" from her container. By calling for a "ten" rather than getting it from the container himself, Mitchell was following one of our rules: only the people with the containers of blocks could actually put them out, to save double dipping.

"Three popped," read Tom. Several hands waved.

"Vanessa," I said. Vanessa removed three "ones".

"How many were left?" asked Tom. All hands were up.

"Trevor," I said.

"Ten." Trevor then packed away the remaining "ten" and we were ready for the next problem to be read.

The children were very interested in the process of exchanging and several of them wrote problems specifically for the purpose of exchanging "hundreds" for "tens" and then "tens" for "ones".

PENGUINS

600 penguins went tobogganing. 6 crashed. How many were still tobogganing?

500 penguins went swimming. 4 were captured by leopard seals. How many were still swimming?

Stage four: Combining steps

The children began to combine two steps in the process of adding or subtracting. The following excerpt from one problem provides an example.

BUDGIES

I had 34 budgies. For my birthday I got 18 more ...

When the children worked on this problem, many of them suggested that, instead of putting out a "ten" and eight "ones" to represent the eighteen new budgies, two "tens" could be put out, and two "ones" removed.

Here is a subtraction example.

POCKET MONEY

I had $30. I spent $7 ...

To subtract seven from three "tens" already out, the children suggested removing one of the "tens" and replacing it with three "ones".

The children continually refined their computation strategies during the fourth stage. I never modelled or even suggested strategies, but let them arise spontaneously. Jenny's problem, *Fish*, gave rise to an interesting development, as the following dialogue indicates.

Jenny read, "I had fifty fish."

Mitchell put out five "tens".

"Nine died." Several hands were waving.

"Carmen," I said. Carmen returned a "ten" to Mitchell and called for a "one".

"I bought ninety-seven more."

If their usual practice had been followed, the children would have put out a "hundred" and removed three "ones". But this time it was not possible because there were four "tens" and only one "one" out in the middle. The children in charge of the "tens" and "ones" containers were about to put out the necessary blocks when Lisa got up on her knees and waved one hand wildly.

"Lisa?" I asked.

"You can put out a 'hundred' and seven 'ones' and put away one of the 'tens'. You don't have to do all the counting and exchanging then."

Thereafter, most of the children were on the lookout for such moves.

Damien's problem which follows extended the children even further.

"I had five hundred dollars," he read. Liza put out five "hundreds".

"I lost twenty dollars." Vanessa was chosen and she removed one of the "hundreds" and called for eight "tens".

"I got two thousand dollars from Mum." Michael put out two "thousands".

"I lost five cents." Tim's hand waved as he got up onto his knees. A few other hands followed. I waited. More hands went up, more children were on their knees, reaching forwards and jabbing at the air with outstretched arms.

"Yes. Tim?" I asked. Tim returned one of the "tens" to its container and called for nine "ones". Then on a scrap of paper he wrote "95 c".

Later, when it came to, "I lost one cent", Jennifer crossed out the "95 c" and wrote "94 c".

Stage five: Using a range of materials for solving problems

The fifth stage featured the use of a variety of materials to supplement the MAB blocks.

When the children began writing problems containing thousands, we had no MAB "thousands" in our classroom. The children were quick to use anything at hand to represent a thousand. Tins, boxes or single Unifix cubes were used. After a short time a single Unifix cube came to be the accepted representation of a thousand.

One day Tom said to me, "We could make MAB 'thousands' by gluing ten 'hundreds' together and making a big cube". I asked him to go to the Year Three area of the school and ask if he could borrow an MAB "thousand". His head came closer to mine and his eyes gleamed as he said, "They *make* them?" He gave a little excited jump, clapped his hands together and started off towards the Year Three area. He returned shortly afterwards, hiding the block behind his back. By then the class had gathered near me for discussion. Tom furtively passed the block to me. "Make them guess what it is!" he whispered. I held it up. Several voices exclaimed, "It's a 'thousand'!"

A few problems called for the use of tens of thousands and hundreds of thousands. Ten Unifix cubes together were used as "ten thousands" and as we had several tennis-ball tins in the room they were used as "hundred thousands".

In the latter half of Year Two, several children brought other problem-solving materials to the class sessions. These materials included:

- Calculators, when they were available
- An abacus
- Plastic replicas of $1, 10 c and 1c coins
- Unifix cubes which were used in conjunction with sheets of paper, folded into segments. The segments were labelled 1, 10, 100, 1000
- Unifix cubes which were given values according to their relative positions ("ones" to the far right, then "tens" to the left of them etc.)

The children with the MAB blocks were still in control of the problem-solving. The children using other materials worked quietly and checked their answers against the ones found with the MAB blocks.

Stage six: Pencil-and-paper calculations

In the sixth stage, pencil-and-paper calculations became widely used.

Written calculations were first used when we were working on the problem books which ended with the question, "How many in the whole book?" These books featured one problem per page, so the final answer was found by adding the answers on all the previous pages. It was not long before someone suggested writing the answer to each page on the blackboard so that we had a record of them. At each problem-solving session thereafter we appointed a child to be the blackboard recorder. Several of the children then started to bring to the sessions clipboards with paper attached so they could keep their own records of the answers and add them together themselves.

The children developed their own methods of adding, subtracting, multiplying and dividing. I applied the same philosophy to the development of computation skills as to the development of other problem-solving skills, and thus did not demonstrate any standard techniques nor set practice exercises at any stage during the program. I was confident that the children would devise methods of computation when the need for them arose.

Most children's first pencil-and-paper calculations consisted of diagrams rather than standard number symbolism. They drew marks to represent numbers.

Here is a sample problem, and how Mitchell solved it using a pencil-and-paper calculation.

MY TEDDY

I want to buy a teddy and it costs $39. I've saved up $24 so far. How much more do I need to save?

On paper, Mitchell drew this:

Comparing the two number representations, Mitchell said, "There's one more ten here so that's ten dollars she has to get, and there's five more dollars here. So that's fifteen dollars she needs."

Later, the children found that using conventional number symbols was the most efficient means of written computation. Each child devised his or her own ways of using number symbols.

When the children were writing problems which generated lists of numbers, some interesting arrangements of numbers on paper arose. The children were conscious of the need to keep the tens together and the ones together. Some children put the tens on one side of their piece of paper and the ones on the other side. Many children found that by writing the numbers one under the other (as in a standard vertical algorithm) they were, in effect, putting the tens together and the ones together.

Once the numbers had been arranged on the paper, the children had to operate on them in some way. Simple counting was not a common procedure. The children used more sophisticated methods. They "looked for tens" in the ones column and for hundreds in the tens column. This was a popular procedure and the children were able to do it very quickly. The following example shows how the children added a list of numbers arising from one problem.

50	15~~0~~	1~~5~~~~0~~
150	15~~0~~	1~~5~~~~0~~
264	→ 264	→ 264
82	82	1~~8~~2
20	20	~~2~~0
		566

(They did not write the list of numbers three times as is shown above. The three lists show the three stages of working the algorithm.)

The methods the children devised were discussed by the class in the same way as were other problem-solving strategies:

- Why is this a good way to work it out?
- Is there another way?
- Would this work for larger numbers?

INVESTIGATIONS

4

4.1 Organising investigations

Timetabling investigations

The children worked on investigations almost every day. Many were completed in one session, others were longer term and were carried out over several days.

Because investigations were not an addition to a formal mathematics program, but took the place of one, it was not difficult finding time for them.

The first investigations

The earliest investigations were done by the class together as a means of introducing general investigation steps and strategies.

The early topics were diverse:

- Are there more girls or boys in our class?
- What classroom pet will we buy?
- What can you find out about the number six?
- How many different shapes can you make with three sides?
- How can you sort these seeds?

At this early stage I led the children to decide how to do an investigation and how to report their findings. We always began by discussing how the topic could be approached and the children were invited to make lots of suggestions. For example, when comparing the number of girls and boys in the class, I asked the children to find as many ways as they could to show the number of each. This led them to make models, pictures and diagrams.

After the children had discussed their findings we wrote a report of what they had done. These reports included the children's pictures and diagrams.

Later investigations

Later, most investigations were done by individuals or small groups of children.

Sometimes all the children worked on the same topic and compared their results. On the topic "Halves", the children worked alone or in pairs, using water and various containers, Plasticine and a pan balance, paint, pencils, paper and scissors to halve and double. Some children recalled earlier work on symmetry and some children used Unifix cubes to halve numbers. The children wrote reports and shared with each other what they had learned.

Some investigations were done by only one group of children who gathered data from the others in the class. For example, the question, "Are boys stronger than girls?" involved one group devising tests of strength and carrying out the tests with each child in the class. They reported twice to the class. The first time they told the class what they wanted to find out and explained how they would be testing the children. On the second occasion they reported the results of their tests and discussed their conclusion.

4.2 Investigation topics

Sources of topics

There was a wide range of possible investigation topics. They were drawn from all curriculum areas.

Mathematics concepts and skills as a source of topics

Many investigations were set as a means of introducing mathematics skills and concepts to the children. For example, a skill such as using a ruler was introduced and developed in this way. The general question, "How can we use a ruler?" started the children thinking and experimenting.

The children often extended the investigation topics presented. After the early work on using rulers, the children suggested some topics requiring the use of rulers. These topics included "Measuring insects" and "How fast does grass grow?" Some children suggested the topic "Making drawings bigger", which required them to double, treble and quadruple lengths and areas. The children drew small pictures, then drew the same picture two, three or four times larger. Such investigations provided purposeful measurement which led the children to work out how a ruler could be used. No directions or traditional practice exercises were needed for the children to gain competence in measuring.

Other curriculum areas as sources of topics

Curriculum areas other than mathematics were a good source of investigations.

Children's literature provided many topics, particularly related to number concepts. In Kindergarten we investigated the numbers that occur in well-known stories, songs and rhymes such as "The Three Little Pigs", "The Three Bears", "The Three Billy Goats Gruff", "The Three Little Kittens Who Lost Their Mittens", "The Wolf and the Seven Little Kids" and "The Seven Dwarfs". We investigated counting sequences in rhymes and songs. A song about ten fat sausages that go "bang" and "pop" in pairs until they have all gone initiated an investigation of counting in twos. We studied counting books, noting which numbers were commonly found in them, and the ways they were represented. I asked the children what numbers they would put in a counting book, how they would represent them, and why.

In later years we studied the works of authors such as Pat Hutchins, Eric Carle, Pamela Allen, and Mitsumasa and Masaichiro Anno, and we noted their interest in mathematical topics. Many stories led to investigations. We read Ludwig Bemelmans' books about Madeline, in which twelve little girls walk in two straight lines, and we explored other possible arrangements of the twelve girls. Pat Hutchins' book *The Doorbell Rang* (Puffin, 1988) led the children to find other numbers that could be the focus of a similar story. In Margaret Mahy's "Shopping with a Crocodile" (in *Downhill Crocodile Whizz and Other Stories*, Puffin, 1987), we found out that the crocodile had forty-two toothbrushes, and the children worked out ways to represent forty-two. We also found out that, when the crocodile bought his forty-third toothbrush, he needed to start a new toothbrush rack; I set the children the problem of finding out how many toothbrush racks the crocodile already had. Some poems initiated investigations, such as Michael Rosen's "Boy friends", which led to some work on fractions.

Science, social studies and physical education topics provided scope for gathering, representing and interpreting statistics. Many of these topics involved measurement.

In science, for instance, we made a study of woodlice, investigating their size, speed, food and habitat preferences. In the social studies topic "Our Community", questions such as the following gave rise to the collection, representation and interpretation of statistics:

- How are the roads in our suburb used?
- Which time of day is the busiest for the local shops?
- Which facilities in our suburb are used the most?
- Which of the nearby shopping centres is used the most by people in our suburb?
- What is the most common form of transport in our suburb?

Physical education topics were based on the questions: How far?, How fast? and How accurate? The children collected statistics on distance and accuracy of ball throwing; on the number of times they could bounce a ball without stopping; on the comparative speed of running, jumping, skipping, hopping, and so on.

Music and movement inspired some investigations. For instance, the children investigated note values, composing variations of a bar of music with four beats.

Children setting investigation topics

The children and I shared the responsibility of setting topics. Sometimes the children indirectly suggested topics. In their eagerness to make comparisons, they made claims such as, "Boys are stronger than girls" and "I've found the biggest leaf in the playground". Such claims were very useful as the basis for investigations.

At other times the children directly set topics: "What's your favourite vegetable, Mrs Skinner? We're doing an investigation." "I'm going to see what happens when I add seven more to lots of numbers. I'm going to find out what the pattern is."

4.3 Steps in an investigation

Discussing the topic

In the early investigations I guided discussions by asking questions which led the children to suggest ways they could go about the investigation. I intervened as little as possible. As the children gained competence, the guidance I gave was often simply making sure all the children joined in the discussions.

Early in Year One I suggested the topic "Numerals and symmetry". The children weren't quite sure where to start until I suggested they ask some questions to guide their work. They set the following questions: Which single numbers have lines of symmetry? Which double numbers have lines of symmetry? (By "double numbers" they meant two-digit numerals.) Which other numbers have lines of symmetry? (By "other numbers" they meant numerals with more than two digits.) Once the children set the questions, they were able to work in pairs or alone to continue the investigation.

The Year Two topic "Children and television", on which the children worked in groups, generated the following questions: Which is the most popular children's television show? What kind of shows do children like best? How much time do children spend watching television? What kinds of advertisements are on children's television shows? How much time do the advertisements take? What would we do if television hadn't been invented?

Responding to the topic

The children were allowed to respond to investigation topics in their own ways. They made the important decisions as to what action had to be taken and what data was needed. If I had made these decisions, the children's involvement would have been limited to tasks such as measuring and counting.

A wide range of materials was available for the children to use in their investigations. They were not restricted to pencil-and-paper work and often liked using art and craft materials to present their findings.

Reporting on the topic

After investigative work, the children reported their findings to the class. At first they gave verbal reports. In Year Two the children usually wrote reports which included questions they had raised, data they had collected, their analysis of the data and their conclusions.

4.4 Developing concepts and skills through investigations

As the children developed competence with investigations, they also developed a range of other mathematical concepts and skills.

It is possible to present any mathematical topic through investigations. For instance, instead of teaching children to count simply by rote practice, investigations which provide a purpose for counting can be used.

Many mathematical concepts which are usually presented to children in formal lessons arose naturally during investigations. For example, the children spontaneously developed ways of counting, measuring, sampling, averaging, rounding numbers, rating and working algorithms. They used concepts like ratio, and median, mode and mean averages. They did not know the conventional terms for these but they developed a very good understanding of their purpose.

Classification

Classification experiences are basic to the development of concepts and to an understanding of relationships between concepts. For instance, classification experiences are essential to an understanding of the relationships between quadrilaterals, parallelograms, rectangles and squares. I provided many classification activities across the curriculum each year.

These activities required the children to collect, classify, reclassify and label objects. Some of the topics we covered are listed below. Some are general and some are more specific. The more general topics were long-term studies.

- Playground collections
- Sorting people (The children used magazines and newspapers as sources of pictures of people, and they used themselves.)
- Sorting animals
- Sorting words
- Sorting shapes
- Sorting lines
- Sorting numbers
- Making and sorting shapes with four straight sides
- Investigating "In how many ways can you sort the numbers up to twenty?"

The following investigation was an introductory classification activity in Kindergarten.

How can things be sorted?

Each child was asked to find one small object in the playground. The children discussed the range of objects collected.

I suggested we sort the objects and asked for a volunteer. Craig sorted the objects according to type; for example, all the leaves were put together, and all the sticks were put together.

"Can they be sorted in a different way?" I asked. There were some suggestions based on physical attributes of the objects (such as smooth/rough) and we tried those classifications.

Lisa said, "We can put all the nature things together and all the rubbish together." We followed this idea and as the children sorted I looked for something that could be placed in both categories. I found a piece of orange peel. When the children finished their sorting I held up the peel and asked, "Where would you put this?"

The children argued for a while for one or other of the categories before they realised the peel should be placed in both. They decided to create a third category and placed the peel alone between the two other piles.

"So it doesn't belong with any of the other things then?" I asked. Adam said, "I know!", broke the peel into two pieces and put one piece in each pile.

"Is this a good way to do it?" I asked the class. Several thought it was, but some children were not so sure. Corinne said, "Now it looks like that piece of peel is nature and that piece is rubbish."

After they had discussed their problem further, the children decided to push the piles close together so that the peel could be in both piles at the same time.

I produced two pieces of paper to write the labels for the two categories. "I know!" said Lisa, "Put all the rubbish on one piece of paper and all the nature things on the other piece and push the bits of paper together so they cover each other a bit and put the peel on there."

I returned to the original question, "How can things be sorted?", to focus the concluding discussion.

Counting and comparing

Counting was a fundamental mathematical activity at all stages of the program. The earliest counting children did was counting one by one in response to the question, "How many?". Later, the children developed more sophisticated methods of counting, such as grouping in tens, estimating, and rounding off numbers.

Investigations were used to introduce all counting skills. Many investigation topics provided purposeful counting; for example:

- On which day do we have the most lunch orders in our class?
- How many windows do cars have?
- Do all small Smarties packets contain the same number of Smarties?
- How many segments do mandarins have?

More sophisticated counting skills were also explored in investigations, for example:

- Can you arrange a group of objects so that it is easier to count them?
- How can you make a good estimate of a number of objects?
- How many seeds has a pumpkin?
- Can you work out how many children are in our school, without counting them?

The following account is of an investigation done in Kindergarten which provided counting practice. This investigation, like most other counting investigation topics, provided the means to develop concepts other than just counting ones.

Which stairs in our school have the most steps?

Our school had several sets of stairs with up to eight steps in each. I asked the children which set of stairs had the most steps. This was an appropriate investigation for children who were developing concepts of numbers up to ten, as it provided purposeful counting.

By asking "How can we find out?", different strategies could be considered.

The children decided to find all the stairs in the school and count the steps in each. One child suggested we photocopy a plan of the school which was on the classroom wall and mark all the stairs on the map, so that we didn't miss any.

We walked around the school counting steps and drawing each set on a separate piece of paper. When all the information was collected, we discussed the drawings:

"This staircase looks the biggest but it's only got three steps. We drew the steps too big."

"We should draw them all the same size."

"That's too hard."

"We could write the number of steps on them."

"We could make the stairs out of blocks all the same."

They made models of the staircases out of blocks and I showed them how they could dip a block into paint and print pictures of the staircases. Some children printed pictures of all the staircases and wrote the number of steps in each set.

We discussed the results and displayed the pictures with a written record of our findings.

How many sticks can we collect in one minute?

This was a Year One topic that arose when several of the children were interested in collecting sticks in the playground. We collected sticks for one minute and counted the total. As there were over two hundred, there was a lot of counting to be done. We did it together, as I thought it would provide some good counting practice and an exploration of ways to count.

The children decided straight away to group the sticks in tens. I asked them to suggest as many ways as they could to count to ten. They came up with a variety of suggestions:

- Counting rhythmically in twos — 1, 2 … 3, 4 … 5, 6 … 7, 8 … 9, 10
- Singing the song, "One little, two little, three little Indians … "
- Counting backwards
- Counting in other languages
- Mouse counting — "ee, ee-ee, ee-ee-ee, ee-ee-ee-ee … "
- Chanting the rhyme, "1, 2, Buckle my shoe … "
- In words which rhymed with the numbers — "Bun, shoe, tree, door, hive, mix, heaven, plate, shine, hen."

Comparative measurement

The earliest stage of measurement involved making direct comparisons between objects without using units of measurement. Investigations provided purposeful practice in making comparisons. Here are some of the topics we investigated:

- Are six-year-olds taller than five-year-olds?
- Who in our class can take the biggest footstep?
- Do shadows change size?
- Which is fatter — your wrist or your ankle?
- Which can you throw further — a tennis ball or a ping pong ball? (This led to experimentation with other balls.)
- Which are heavier — apples or oranges?
- Which rock is bigger? (I provided two smallish rocks of different dimensions so it was not easy to tell by sight which was bigger. A pair of scales, a bucket of water, paper, lengths of string and some Plasticine were also provided.)

A Kindergarten investigation on smiles was very popular.

Who has the biggest smile in our class?

One morning I said, "I wonder who has the biggest smile in our class." The children forced wide smiles and looked around at each other. Several of them made guesses.

"How can we find out?" I asked.

"We could measure them."

"How?" I asked.

After a few suggestions, the children decided to use strips of paper which they could cut into lengths according to the size of their smiles. They also decided to work in pairs as they thought it was too difficult to measure on their own.

"What will you do with the strips of paper?" I asked. They liked one child's idea of pasting them on a large sheet of paper.

A table was set up with all the necessary materials and the children spent the morning taking turns to measure, cut and paste. By the end of the session they had pasted, haphazardly over the sheet of paper, thirty paper strips, each one labelled with a name.

In the follow-up discussion I held up the sheet of paper and again asked, "Who has the biggest smile?" The children began guessing.

"You're guessing," I said. "How can you work it out? Is it helpful to have all these paper strips pasted down?"

"No, because you have to have the strips together to see which one sticks out the most," said Sam. He and a friend rearranged the strips. They drew a line across another sheet of paper, cut out the strips and pasted them so one end of each was on the line. Sam found that he in fact had the biggest smile, and before he showed the class the second sheet of paper he wrote on it, "I Hfv the biGst sloll."

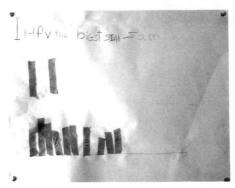

Informal measurement

Informal measurement involved using arbitrary units of measurement to make comparisons.

There were two stages of using informal measurement. In the first stage, the children used measures such as shells, stones and footsteps to make rough comparisons.

In the second stage, they realised the need to standardise their units of measure. When we did an investigation, "Who has the furthest distance to go from their front door to their letterbox?", the children initially decided that each would measure the distance according to footsteps. They quickly suggested that was "unfair" (as they put it) because the children took different-sized footsteps. So they measured one child's footstep with a length of string and each child cut a piece of string the same length to use.

Similarly, when the children wanted to compare the masses of their shoes, they devised a standard mass by wrapping a group of tiny stones in foil. Other foil packets of stones were made and standardised by balancing each one against the original.

The children used their standardised units of measurement to investigate topics such as the following:

- How big is your hand?
- Doubling area (The children used Unifix cubes for measuring area.)
- Quadrupling area
- Who has the tallest mum?

Standard measurement

In Year Two the children progressed to using standard metric units of measurement.

Many investigation topics provided purposeful measurement; for example:
- Are boys heavier than girls?
- What is the shortest route from our classroom to the library?
- Which classroom in the school is the biggest?
- How long is a finger?
- Are the tallest people the heaviest?
- Whose drink bottle can hold the most drink?

The five investigations which follow outline in some detail what the children did, to illustrate the way they developed a range of concepts through investigations.

Which colour pencil is used the most in this class?
One of the children suggested this as a topic. In the introductory discussion we talked about how the children could go about finding out.

"We can look at the drawings people do."

"We can get people to keep a piece of paper and draw each colour on it when they use it."

"We can ask each person which one they use the most."

"We can measure the pencils and see which ones are used up the most."

These suggestions were discussed and the children decided to follow the last one. They worked in small groups to measure a tin of pencils and record their findings in any way they chose.

One group drew lines the length of each pencil and wrote the colour names on the lines. Some groups wrote the measurements using the colour pencil they were measuring. Three groups organised their measurements in some way: one of them measured all the pencils of one colour first and kept those measurements together; another group listed the pencils from shortest to longest; the third group made a graph with measurements at half-centimetre intervals along the top of their paper and blocks of colour representing the pencils under the relevant measurement.

The class discussed the various methods of representing the information and decided to collate all the information and represent it in the form of a graph, as the last group had done. A group of children collated all the information and presented the final graph to the class for discussion.

Project Pinocchio

Project Pinocchio was concerned with the question, "Do noses keep on growing?"

The class suggested the following ways of finding out.

"Measure your nose now and when you're older."

"Each day you measure your nose."

"No, each year."

"That would take too long to find out."

"Measure our noses and then measure Mrs Skinner's nose."

"All people the same age mightn't have the same size noses. Just like some people are tall and some are short."

"Measure brothers' and sisters' noses."

"I saw a picture of my Mum's nose when she was a baby. I could look at photos of Mum when she was a teenager."

"We could get pictures out of magazines."

The last suggestion was popular and I asked for volunteers to work on the task. When the group reported back to the class they said that looking at pictures was not much use because the people in the pictures were different sizes; some were close to the camera and some were far away.

The children then decided to measure the noses of people of different ages. "How do you measure a nose?" asked one child. "You can't get it exactly because it's not a straight line."

The children suggested some ways of measuring a nose. They decided that it didn't matter exactly how it was done, as long as it was done the same way each time. Several of the children measured the noses of their family members. Angela's work is one example:

Noses

Noses can be short and big.

Noses can be long and skinny.

Mum's nose is three and a half centimetres long.

Dad's nose is five and a half centimetres long.

Peter's nose is two and three quarter centimetres long.

Kelly's nose is four centimetres long.

My nose is three centimetres long.

Michael's nose is four and a half centimetres long.

The children collected all the statistics and grouped the measurements according to the age of the people measured.

One child concluded, "Bodies keep on growing and then they stop. Noses are just the same."

Do heads grow?

Shortly after Project Pinocchio had been completed, the toddler brother of one of the children visited the classroom with his mother. One child called out, "Hey, he's got a big head for a baby. It's nearly as big as Mrs Skinner's."

The children were very interested and someone suggested we investigate heads as we had noses.

One group of children took up the idea. They drew around the toddler's body as he lay on a large sheet of paper. Then they drew around me for a comparison.

When they were painting the drawings they had made, they noticed that the toddler's head took up a large part of his body. They worked out that it was about a quarter the size of his body. They looked at the drawing of me and worked out that my head was about a seventh of my total body.

By this time the group were worried that something was wrong with their classmate's brother, so I suggested they look at other babies too. They found pictures of babies in magazines and worked out the proportion of their heads to their bodies. They were fascinated, and went on to look at pictures of people of various ages in order to do the same comparisons for them.

The children were interested in the fact that for this investigation, the magazine pictures were useful, unlike for the earlier investigations of noses.

When the group showed their work to the class, they reported their conclusion that heads don't grow as much as bodies because they don't need to — they start off pretty big!

Are boys' feet or girls' feet bigger?

The children began by measuring the area of their feet and listing the measurements on two sheets of paper, one for the girls and one for the boys. The children added all the measurements in each list. The girls' total was more, but no one accepted that as fair.

"There are more girls!" said one boy.

"Cross off some of the girls' measurements so we've got the same number of each," suggested another boy.

"Which ones?" asked someone else.

They suggested a few ways it could be done, but none was deemed fair. Then came the suggestion:

"Let's put all the measurements in order on each sheet of paper and find out which is the biggest foot on each list."

When that was done, someone suggested we compare the biggest size and the smallest size in each list.

"Let's find the one in the middle too, because that's the fair one," suggested one of the girls.

The complete lists looked like this:

	Boys	Girls
Big	171 sq cm	150 sq cm
Middle	152 sq cm	127 sq cm
Small	128 sq cm	100 sq cm

There was no argument with the conclusion that the boys' feet were bigger than the girls' feet.

Are boys heavier than girls?

Here is the report of this investigation carried out by one group of Year Two children.

"The first thing we did was get some people out of our class. Then we measured how heavy they were."
(Class list attached to the report with each child listed alphabetically and their mass recorded beside their names.)

"Then we put all the measurements in order from heaviest to lightest."
(Boys on one list and girls on another.)

"We got the middle of each list or average to be fair. In our class the girls are heavier than the boys. But that is only in our class that is. So we are getting some more people."
(Same procedure with class lists and ordered lists with another Year Two class.)

"The girls are the heaviest again so we are going to try with some older children."
(Same procedure with some Year Five and Six classes. When there was an even number of children on a list the group took the middle two measurements and worked out the number midway between them.)

"We found out that girls are heavier than boys. We thought when boys grow up they might be heavier than girls because they will have more muscles than girls. We are going to measure some adults."
(The group then recorded the mass of several adults in the school, ordered the measurements of males and females, and marked the middle measurement on each list, as they did with the children.)

"We found out that men are heavier than women."

Statistics

Statistical investigations involved gathering data in response to a question. Several of these involved measurement and were discussed in the three preceding sections. Here the focus is investigations not involving measurement.

Some of the topics we explored were:

- What is the most common bird in our playground?
- What is the most common insect in this shrub?
- How many seeds are in an apple?
- How do children spend their time?
- How did our grandparents spend their time when they were children?
- Children and sleep
- Children and television
- Children and food

Here is the report written by a group of children after they investigated Smarties.

How do Smarties get in their boxes?

"Mrs Skinner asked us, 'We know how Smarties get out of the Smartie boxes, but how do they get in?'

We thought perhaps machines would count the Smarties into the boxes but we didn't know if they counted in some of each colour or just counted in a whole lot of colours all mixed up.

We counted the Smartie colours. There were different numbers of each colour. Some boxes didn't have all the colours. So that means they weren't put in in a sequence. So a machine must have mixed up the Smarties and just dropped them in. They didn't even put in the same number of Smarties. They just did it, as long as it has a mass of about 25 grams.

Do you sometimes feel that it's unfair if you like the blues best and there's only one or two blues in a pack? We wanted to make a fair box of Smarties.

We found out which colour we liked the most and what order we liked the Smartie colours. We each rated the colours and we added these up.

This is the order we liked the colours: blue, purple, pink, red, yellow, orange, green and brown. We wished that there could be 8 blue, 7 purple, 6 pink, 5 red, 4 yellow, 3 orange, 2 green and 1 brown in a Smartie packet.

We want to make a machine that puts 36 Smarties in a packet. 36 is a triangular number. The mass of the packet would be about 35 grams."

Probability

The children developed their first ideas about probability from two games we created.

Rosie's Walk

We made this game based on Pat Hutchins' book, *Rosie's Walk* (Macmillan, 1968). The children made models of the buildings and other features in the story. When they put these together to make a three-dimensional map, Kate suggested we make it into a game. We added stepping stones through the map for Rosie and the fox to walk on. The children decided that Rosie and the fox would proceed along the stepping stones as two players took turns to throw a die. The game evolved through trial and error, so that the fox started on the first stepping stone and Rosie started on the sixth stone, and Rosie moved first. The aim of the game was to see how often Rosie got home in time for dinner, and how often the fox caught her. As a pair of children finished a game, they recorded whether or not Rosie got home. The children kept comparing the number of times Rosie got home with the number of times she was caught. Because Rosie had a head start, the children thought that Rosie would reach home on more occasions than she was caught.

Tim's game

Tim pasted onto a sheet of cardboard nineteen coloured paper squares to make a picture of a dinosaur. He also made a die from a box. On each of two faces of the die he put a square, and on the other faces he put a hexagon, a triangle, a rectangle and a circle. He provided fifteen red Unifix cubes and fifteen green Unifix cubes. Two players, one with the red cubes and one with the green cubes, took turns to throw the die; if a square showed, the player put one of his or her Unifix cubes on a square of the dinosaur. When all of the dinosaur squares were occupied, the players compared the number of cubes each one had put out. The one with the most cubes out was the winner.

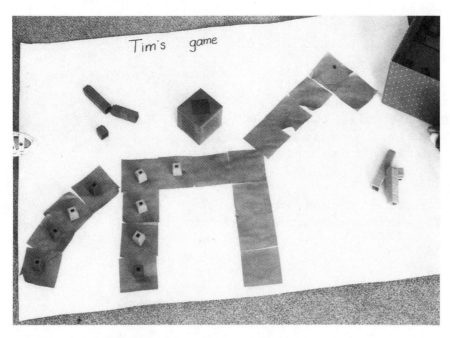

The children became very interested in the fact that the final tally of cubes was usually ten to nine, and sometimes eleven to eight. Only very rarely was there a different result.

So, quite spontaneously, the children were developing ideas about probability. I extended this by setting some investigation topics, such as the following:

- Investigating coin tossing
- Investigating dice throwing
- Put nine black Unifix cubes and one red Unifix cube in a box; investigate the chance of drawing out the red cube.

The work on probability gave the children opportunities to learn more about statistics. They were collecting, representing and interpreting data, and they were gaining an understanding of the idea of a reasonable sample. We didn't use the word "probability", though the children's spontaneous language included the words "chance" and "probable".

Shape

Investigating shape focused on making, classifying and naming shapes. Our topics included the following:

- Shapes with three straight sides
- Making triangles
- Making squares with Logo on the computer
- Square corners
- Numerals and symmetry
- What shapes are most commonly used in buildings, and why.

The following accounts of investigations demonstrate the work we did in Year One (the work on squares) and Year Two (the work on octagons).

Asking questions about squares

In a lot of our investigative work I encouraged the children to pose questions for others. When they worked in groups on the topic of squares, they produced the following questions. These questions then became the focus of further investigative work.

- How can you make a square starting from a circle?
- How many little squares can you use to make a big square? (There are lots of answers, so stop at 100 or you'll go on for ever. It never stops.)
- How many ways can you cut a square in half and in quarters?
- How can you make a square from two triangles and what kind of triangles do you need?
- What is a square?
- How can you make a square out of a corner of a piece of paper?
- How do you make the biggest square you can from a piece of computer paper?

Making regular octagons

We began by discussing how a regular octagon would look. The children were familiar with the term "polygon" and were able to work out what an octagon would be. I had to help them to figure out the meaning of "regular". They were asked to discuss, in pairs, what "regular" meant, and what that might tell them about a regular polygon. The pairs reported to the class.

"Regular means you do things at the same time."

"It probably means 'the same'."

"A regular polygon might be one with the same size sides."

I asked, "What about the corners?"

"They'd be the same too."

The children used various materials to construct octagons. These included the Logo program on the classroom computer, paper, hammers, nails and wool, matchsticks and popsticks.

I suggested they try drawing octagons by starting with a simpler shape. A few children thought a square would be a useful starting point as it had half the number of sides and corners as an octagon. They devised two ways of using squares to make octagons.

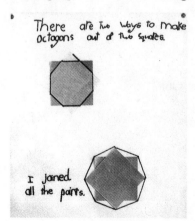

There are two ways to make octagons out of two squares.

I joined all the points.

In the concluding discussion the children displayed their octagons and explained their methods of working. I focused the discussion with the question, "What are the steps everybody had to take, no matter what materials they used?" The children decided that they had needed to make eight equal sides and then place them so that the corners were all the same size. This had been far easier to achieve with three-dimensional materials than with drawing and computer Logo, because the use of three-dimensional materials allowed them to start with eight objects and arrange them by trial and error. With Logo and drawing, the children had to plan their work.

Later, the children made other regular polygons (pentagons, hexagons, heptagons, nonagons and decagons) and suggested what they might be called.

Time

Time investigations centred on timing actions and using clocks. Our topics included:

- Telling the time on a one-handed clock
- Telling the time on a two-handed clock
- Telling the time on a three-handed clock
- Why are there sixty seconds in a minute and sixty minutes in an hour?
- Measuring time
- How to use a stopwatch
- Which is faster — hopping or jumping?

Telling the time on a one-handed clock

I made a model of an analogue clock with only one hand to teach the children to tell the time. If the hand pointed to three, it was three o'clock; if it pointed halfway between three and four, it was half past three; if it was almost at four, it was a few minutes before four o'clock; and so on.

When I introduced the clock, I set the topic, "How could you use a clock with one hand to tell the time?" Most children made very competent use of the clock. Others needed further direction, by means of questions like "How could you show it was five o'clock?", "What about seven o'clock?", "What if it was just after seven o'clock?"

How far can you run in one second?

Here is a record of the children's discussion of this topic.
"Use a stopwatch."
I asked them how.
"Call out 'go' and after one second call out 'stop'."
"What if you're in the air and one second is up?"
"It's hard to stop the watch after one second."
"You can't stop running straight away."
"Run a bit. Call out 'start'. Then call out 'finish'."
"You can't really run your fastest because it's too short to run."
"You can get your speed up in longer runs only."
"Run for a hundred seconds and find a hundredth of it."
"Run for ten seconds and find a tenth of it."
"Run for five seconds and find a fifth of it."
"Run for eight seconds and get an eighth of it."
"Run for two seconds and halve it."

"Or run for three seconds and third it."

I said, "You seem to like the idea of running a distance and then finding a fraction of the time. How can we find out which distance is the best one to run?"

"Go outside and try them out."

So we did, and the children found that the most practical way to measure how far they could run in one second was to measure how far they could run in two seconds, and halve that.

Numbers

Number investigations were the principal means of learning about numbers and number relationships. A full account of number investigations appears in the next two sections of this book, Understanding Numbers and Investigating Numbers.

The following description of one of the Kindergarten number investigations will illustrate how number investigations used the same framework as other investigations.

Wheel numbers

The topic heading "Wheel numbers" was set and I asked the children what they thought I meant them to do. They all thought they should list vehicles and write the number of wheels on each.

"Why?" I asked. "What are you trying to find out?" The children talked about this for a while and decided they were going to find out "what numbers wheels come in". They clarified what they meant by explaining that "shoes come in twos and socks come in twos but wheels come in different numbers".

The children worked in groups of six to list vehicles according to the number of wheels they had. The initial discussion led the children to present their information in some order, as they were directing their attention to the task they had set themselves.

One child suggested looking for pictures of vehicles in magazines. Her group did this and noted that cars and trucks were often pictured side-on, showing only half the wheels. Two children developed this observation into an investigation. They collected such pictures and wrote captions like, "2 is half of 4".

When the groups reported their findings to the class there was some discussion about combining vehicles to create other wheel numbers. A car pulling a trailer would have six wheels, for example; and a combination of one car towing another car would have eight wheels. This led into an investigation of how many wheel numbers could be created by combinations.

Another investigation derived from this one was, "How many ways can we make six wheels?" The children listed combinations of vehicles such as three bicycles or two tricycles.

UNDERSTANDING NUMBERS

5

5.1 Understanding our number system

Our number system relies on four basic concepts which children must understand. These four concepts are:

- successive grouping
- base ten grouping
- place value
- symbolism.

I presented these basic concepts through problems, investigations and games.

Successive grouping

Successive grouping is what we do when we group in tens, then combine ten of those tens to form a hundred, then combine ten hundreds to form a thousand, and so on.

Successive grouping need not be restricted to grouping in tens. Children may gain a better understanding of the concept if they also have experience of grouping in other numbers.

Successive grouping investigations

Our investigations focused on numbers in bases other than ten. One of the children taught us to count to twenty in her native Cambodian. The children investigated the sequence of numbers and found it was a base five system (at least as far as twenty). They invented concrete, visual and written representations of the numbers.

Successive grouping problems

Each successive grouping problem was presented as an incomplete sequence of objects or pictures. The children had to work out what would be the next object or picture in the sequence. We made some sequences of pictures into books. Here is one sequence presented:

CLOUDS

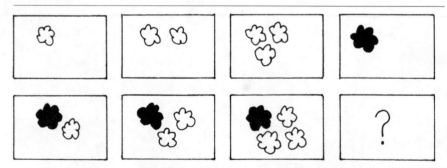

The children worked out that a black cloud represented four white clouds, and that the next picture would have two black clouds and no white clouds.

As a variation of the problems based on incomplete sequences of pictures, the children were sometimes given a set of pictures which they had to put in order. The children also made sets of pictures for others to sequence.

Successive grouping games

Early successive grouping games

Here is a successive grouping game that the children played in their first year at school. The only prerequisite skills were one-to-one correspondence and counting up to five.

Freckles

Materials:
- At least 11 "freckles" (brown counters)
- At least 11 "fingers" (made from pieces of felt)
- One "hand" (made from a piece of felt)
- A die marked 1, 2, 3, ●, ●●, ●●●

Procedure:
The players take turns to throw the die and pick up the number of freckles corresponding to the number shown. When a player has 5 freckles, they are exchanged for a finger; 5 fingers are exchanged for the hand. The player with the hand is the winner.

Later successive grouping games

The children did not play successive grouping games only in Kindergarten. Here are examples of a type of game, introduced in Year One, which reinforced the children's understanding of the concept of successive grouping.

Spiderweb

(A game with base eight numbers)

Materials:
- A "spiderweb" (a piece of felt, about 80 cm x 50 cm, with a spiderweb stitched on)
- About 100 "bugs" (MAB "ones")
- 8 brown Cuisenaire rods (8 cm long), which the children call "sticks"
- A few groups of 8 brown Cuisenaire rods glued together side by side, which the children call "squares"

Procedure:
The first player tosses the bugs onto the spiderweb. Those bugs which do not land on the web are returned to their container. The bugs which do land on the web are counted "as a spider might count them, in eights". Each group of 8 bugs is exchanged for a stick. If the player gets 8 sticks they are exchanged for a square. The player then records his or her total.

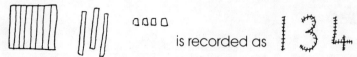

is recorded as 1 3 4

(A child suggested the numbers be written to look like hairy spider legs "so we know it's not really 134 in our numbers.")

The second player goes through the same process. The player with the highest total is the winner.

Triceratops' dinner   ❖

(The dinosaur Triceratops, which had three horns, may have grouped in threes. It had a very small brain so it would not have been able to recognise many number symbols!)

Materials:
- A "swamp" (made from blue felt)
- About 45 "plants" (MAB "ones" dyed green)
- About 15 "sticks" (light-green Cuisenaire rods)
- About 5 "squares" (each one made by gluing 3 sticks side by side)
- A "block" (made by gluing together 3 squares to form a cube)

Procedure:
Each player takes turns to throw the plants onto the swamp. The plants which land off the swamp are returned to their container. The ones which land on the swamp are counted in threes. Three plants are exchanged for a stick, 3 sticks for a square and 3 squares for a block. The players record their totals.

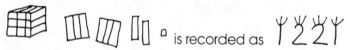

is recorded as ΥᏉᏉΥ

(The 3 lines on each number represented Triceratops' 3 horns.)

Base ten grouping

When the children were familiar with the concept of successive grouping and could confidently count to ten, I introduced many games, problems and investigations focusing on base ten grouping.

Base ten grouping problems

The problems focused on counting objects and representing numbers. To count efficiently and to represent numbers effectively, the children decided to group objects in tens.

We devised a range of "How many?" problems. Each problem took the form of a question, with a concrete model of the answer supplied. The children had to group and count the objects in the concrete model and answer the questions verbally. Here are some examples:

- How many bones are there in a human foot? (Twenty-six white Unifix cubes were supplied by the child who posed the question.)

- How many days has the month of May? (I put out thirty-one cards, each with a day of the week written on it.)
- How old is Mrs Skinner? (I put out thirty-five birthday candles.)
- How many eggs are there per carton? (The child who posed this question put a paper "egg" in each segment of an egg carton.)

Next, problems requiring them to make concrete or visual representations of numbers were introduced. Here are some of the topic questions:

- How can we keep a record of the number of days our caterpillar will stay in its cocoon?
- How many days will it take a bunch of leaves to turn brown?
- How can we make a picture to show there were ninety-two people on board the *Endeavour*?

The children loved this work and found many opportunities to represent numbers. Tom came to school one day and told me his great-great-grandmother was ninety-four years old. "Can I make a picture to show how old she is and then everyone else can work it out?" he asked. He had a friend paint the palms of his hands and then he printed them nine times onto a sheet of paper. He added prints of four fingers to complete the picture.

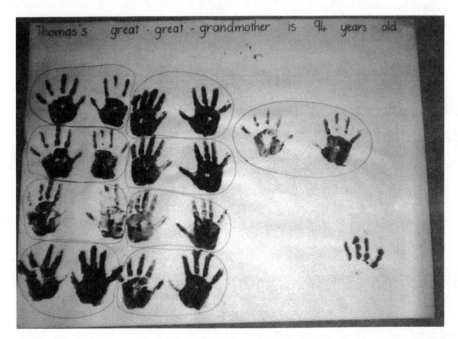

A few days later Tom found a stick in the playground and came into the classroom after lunch, wobbling and leaning on the stick. In a quavering voice he said, "I'm a very old man." "How old are you, Tom?" I asked. "Ninety-seven," he replied. Another child suggested making a picture to show how old Tom was. They came up with the idea of representing each ten with a picture of a birthday cake with ten candles. For each one, they made a picture of a cupcake with one candle. On the picture they wrote:

"Thomas is a very old man. He has a walking stick. He wobbles. Adam helps him walk. Felicia holds his back up. Thomas is ninety-seven years old. And guess what! He is only in Year One!"

Another type of problem which provided experience with tens and ones was the "Guess which number?" problem. Vanessa originated the idea like this:

MY MUM

My mum is thirty something. How old is my mum?

The other children made appropriate guesses and Vanessa responded by telling them whether the answer was more or less than each guess.

Base ten grouping investigations

The investigation topics included:

- Why do we group in tens?
- How might the first people have represented numbers?
- Our money system
- How are the names for the numbers above ten like the names of the numbers from one to nine?
- How are Spanish number names like our number names, and how are they different? (We teach Spanish at our school.)
- How are French number names like Spanish number names?
- Egyptian number symbols (A system of base ten grouping without place value.)

Base ten grouping games

Washing day

Materials:
- The box in which the game is stored has a "clothesline" drawn along each long side. Ten socks are pictured along each clothesline.
- 20 regular clothespegs
- 24 miniature pegs
- A regular die

Procedure:
The two players take turns to throw the die. On each throw a player collects the number of miniature pegs corresponding to the number showing on the die. When a player has ten miniature pegs they are exchanged for a regular peg which is then pegged onto the first sock on that player's clothesline. The first player to fill his or her line is the winner.

Cherries, apples and watermelon

Materials:
- 24 "cherries" (each made from two pieces of felt, stitched together and filled)
- 24 "apples" (made in the same way)
- A slice of watermelon (made in the same way)
- A regular die

Procedure:
The two players take turns to throw the die. On each throw a player collects the number of cherries corresponding to the number showing on the die. When a player has ten cherries they are exchanged for an apple. Ten apples are exchanged for the slice of watermelon. The player with the watermelon is the winner.

Jellybeans and licorice sticks

This game introduced the children to MAB blocks

Materials:
- About 30 "jellybeans" (MAB "ones", dyed various colours with food colouring)
- 24 "licorice sticks" (MAB "tens", coloured black)
- A "block of chocolate" (an MAB "hundred", coloured brown)
- A regular die

Procedure:
The two players take turns to throw the die. On each throw a player collects the number of jellybeans corresponding to the number showing on the die. When a player has 10 jellybeans they are exchanged for a licorice stick. Ten licorice sticks are exchanged for the block of chocolate. The winner is the player with the block of chocolate.

Dinosaur footprints

Materials:
- 40 "dinosaur footprints", made from flat pieces of cardboard in the shape of dinosaur footprints and labelled with dots to represent the numbers 1 to 40. The dots are grouped in tens where appropriate. For example, 24 is represented as

Procedure:
The children make a trail of dinosaur footprints in order from the first to the fortieth. (This game does not produce a winner.)

Dinosaur bones

Materials:
- 50 "dinosaur bones" (made from flat pieces of white carboard and numbered 1, 2, 3, 4, 5, 6, 7, 8, 9, 10, 10 + 1, 10 + 2, 10 + 3 … 40 + 9, 50)

Procedure:
The children construct the dinosaur skeleton by placing the bones in order from 1 to 50. This game does not produce a winner. The children liked to set up the dinosaur skeleton and the dinosaur footprints together.

Tens and ones toss

Materials:
- A square of felt (about 25 cm by 25 cm) with a different coloured circle (diameter about 8 cm) stitched onto the middle
- A Unifix cube
- 20 plastic straws
- 20 counters

Procedure:
Two players take turns to toss the Unifix cube onto the felt square. If the cube lands in the circle, the player wins a straw (worth 10 points). If the cube lands outside the circle, the player wins a counter (worth 1 point). If the counter lands off the felt, the player doesn't score. The first player to accumulate 100 points is the winner.

Place value

Place value refers to the conventional positioning of numerals to denote value. The concept of place value was introduced through investigations. The children gained further experience with place value conventions through problems and games.

Place value investigations

Here are some of our investigation topics:

- How can we use number symbols instead of pictures to show numbers?
- Is the Egyptian number system a good system?
- Four-and-twenty blackbirds: how has the presentation of numbers changed?
- Do we need rules about how to write numbers?
- How do you know that 23 is twenty-three and not thirty-two?
- Is zero important?

Place value problems

The problems were an extension of the base ten grouping problems. Instead of answering a "How many?" question verbally, with concrete materials or in pictures, the children answered in writing, using numerals.

There were many possibilities for "How many?" problems. They included:

- How many of the children in our class are at school today? (The children decided to keep an attendance record over a month to see how many days we had all the children present.)
- How many glasses of milk can a cow produce in a day? (This required book research.)
- How many weeks are there in a year? (We used calendars.)
- How many teeth do children have?
- How many times can you bounce a ball without stopping? Do you get better with practice?

Place value games

Games such as the following one helped children to gain familiarity with written two-digit numbers.

Toss the pancakes

Materials:
- Several "pancakes" (cut from yellow cardboard), each with a two-digit number on one side.

Procedure:
Each player in turn tosses the pancakes and lets them fall to the floor. The player determines which number showing is the highest. The next player does the same, and the two players compare their highest numbers to find the winner.

Symbolism

Nothing inherently links the written symbols for numbers and operations with what they represent. For example, only convention links the numeral 7 with seven objects.

Symbolism investigations

Through investigations, the children explored the concept of number symbolism.

In dance lessons, for example, the children created sequences of movements and investigated the use of drawings to keep a record of the sequences.

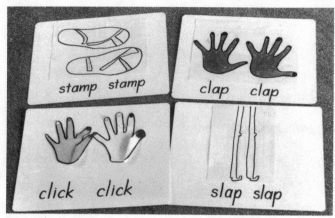

A movement pattern based on 4 twos devised for
"Investigating 8".

In music lessons, the children investigated making written records of sound patterns, creating symbols for sounds such as clapping, stamping and drum beats.

The first symbols the children drew were closely related to what they were representing. For example, a pair of hands symbolised clapping, a pair of feet symbolised stamping, and a drum symbolised a drum beat.

Some children spontaneously simplified their symbols to save time, space and effort. For movements and sounds that were difficult to represent, children investigated making arbitrary choices of symbols: a click of the fingers, for instance, was represented by a small cross.

When investigating the symbols as a means of communication, the class adopted certain symbols as standard for their use.

$\times$ = a click of the fingers

$\vee$ = a handclap

$\llcorner$ = a foot stamping

Symbolism games

Portholes

❖

Materials:
- 12 cards with the following pictures:
  - A boat with 1 porthole
  - A boat with 1 porthole and a fish
  - A boat with 1 porthole and a fish and a seagull
  - A boat with 2 portholes
  - A boat with 2 portholes and a fish
  - A boat with 2 portholes and a fish and a seagull
  - A boat with 3 portholes
  - A boat with 3 portholes and a fish
  - A boat with 3 portholes and a fish and a seagull
  - A boat with 4 portholes
  - A boat with 4 portholes and a fish
  - A boat with 4 portholes and a fish and a seagull

Procedure:
The cards are placed face down on the floor. The teacher asks, "Which one has a boat with one porthole?"

When the children realise it is impossible to work out, they are then asked to help think of some clues to draw on the back of each card, so that they can work out what is on the front. The children then devise symbols to go on the back of the cards.

The children with whom I played this game represented a boat with one porthole by a dot, two portholes by a line, three portholes by a triangle and four portholes by a square. If a card had a fish on it, they drew a ring around the portholes symbol. If a card had a seagull as well as a fish, they drew two rings around the portholes symbol.

Thereafter, when the children used the cards, they placed them face down and directed each other to pick up certain cards. They referred to the symbols on the back to work out which card they were looking for.

The children made many games using symbolism in the same way as the portholes game. Clinton's game is one example.

Clinton's game

❖

Materials:
- A sequence of 6 cards (see overleaf). The symbol on the back of each card appears beside the picture on the card.

Procedure:
This is a game for one player. The cards are placed face down on a flat surface. The player must find the first card in the sequence, then the second, and so on, until the sequence is complete.

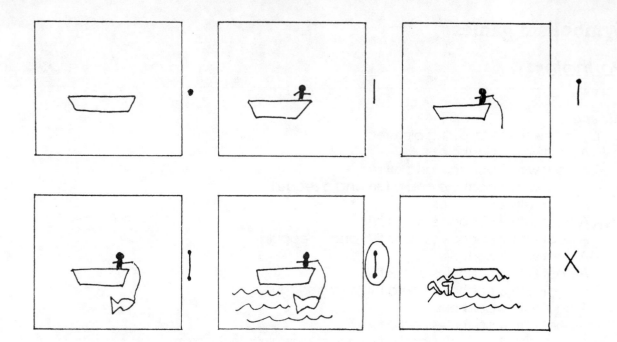

Number system models

Written numerals are an abstract representation of numbers. Before children are ready to work with the written model of numbers they need to have experiences with concrete and visual models.

In my program the children developed concepts of our number system in three stages. They moved from working with concrete representations (such as blocks) to visual representations (such as drawings of blocks) and finally to the abstract conventional number symbols.

Even though the children could recognise and write conventional number symbols from Kindergarten, we did the significant mathematical work (problem solving and investigation) with concrete and visual models of numbers. The use of abstract symbols in the third stage was strongly tied to concrete and visual models.

Concrete models

The children's earliest problem solving was done using the coloured Unifix cubes as concrete representations of objects. Later the children used MAB blocks as a more sophisticated concrete model of the number system. The children also used their fingers as a concrete model of numbers.

Visual models

I noted that the most mathematically competent children in the class had developed in their minds strong visual models of numbers. I wanted all the children to develop such models.

I encouraged the children to create models of numbers on paper. When I worked with children individually I sometimes gave them a problem to solve and asked them to use pencil and paper to work it out.

At first the children drew pictures to represent numbers, then progressed to drawing arbitrary marks. They began by making a mark for each object; later they drew different symbols for ones and tens. Commonly, they used crosses or short lines to represent ones and longer lines or small circles to represent tens. Later, they represented hundreds by large circles or by squares.

The children gradually lost their dependence on drawn images of numbers and developed mental images. We discussed their mental pictures often. These images helped the children considerably with mental calculations.

Abstract model

The abstract model of our number system uses the conventional number symbols.

I did not hurry the children through the transition to this stage and we made strong links between concrete, visual and abstract models. The abstract number symbols were useful for children only when they had a strong visual image of numbers.

When the children found conventional number symbols to be the most efficient way to record and work with numbers, they used them for their problem solving.

INVESTIGATING NUMBERS

6

6.1 Investigating patterns

Pattern, when applied to numbers, is the ordered arrangement of objects, and is a basic mathematical concept. In the program, pattern was fundamental to the children's initial number recognition and to all subsequent number knowledge, as it helped children to form visual images of numbers. For example, eight could be visualised as two fours. This led to efficient written and mental calculation when solving problems.

The children's pattern work took two forms:

- They arranged a particular number of objects, usually in regular patterns. For example, six objects could be arranged as three twos, two threes, or a staircase.
- They made repeating patterns. For example, a pattern based on the number two may have had two red blocks followed by two yellow blocks, then two red blocks, then two yellow blocks, and so on.

Pattern exploration was the basis for the children's investigations of numbers and number relationships. It was also an important aspect of solving many puzzle problems.

Arranging objects

In Kindergarten, the children had to learn about numbers in two fundamental ways. They had to learn conventional number names and numerals, matching them to sets of objects; they had to develop concrete and visual models of numbers.

To learn number names and symbols, the children had to practise them by rote. Rhymes, songs, and movement activities enhanced the rote learning. Providing a purpose for counting, such as setting an investigation topic requiring counting, further enhanced the rote learning.

More significant than this rote learning was the children's investigation of number patterns. It was more important for the children to recognise various ordered arrangements of a number than to recognise the numeral representing that number.

In their investigations, the children made patterns with toys, blocks, Unifix cubes, pegs on pegboards, beads, coins, art materials, food, sounds, movements and their fingers.

Their pattern work helped the children gain familiarity with numbers and number relationships (e.g. eight is one less than nine, two threes are six, if you put three and four together you get seven). This familiarity was fundamental to understanding addition, subtraction, multiplication and division.

I focused the children's attention on their increasing familiarity with number patterns by setting investigation topics such as "How can you recognise six objects without counting them?" Later topics dealt with larger numbers.

Regular patterns

The children were fascinated by the regular patterns which arose when they explored ordered arrangements of objects.

One of the first patterns they made was the "staircase" or triangular pattern which they built up with one block in the first row, two blocks in the second row, three in the third, and so on. Thus they found triangular numbers such as one, three, six, ten and fifteen.

They made square numbers by forming squares with one row of one block, two rows of two blocks, three rows of three blocks, and so on.

They found that any number was a rectangular number because any number of blocks could be placed in one row to form a rectangle. What became interesting was the number of different rectangles that could be made from a particular number of blocks. For instance, with twelve blocks, three rows with four in each row made a rectangle, six rows with two in each row made another rectangle, and one row with twelve in it made a third rectangle.

The children similarly made cubic numbers and pyramid numbers. Occasionally, they would use non-conventional terms to describe patterns they generated, like "chain numbers" which were based on a unit of three.

Repeating patterns

In addition to ordered arrangements of a particular number of objects, the children made repeating patterns based on a particular number.

For example, when studying patterns based on three, a Kindergarten child might have made a pattern by pasting down three coloured paper squares, followed by three triangles, three rectangles, and so on. This would reinforce the child's counting to three and his or her instant recognition of three.

Counting sequences

The children progressed from counting in ones to counting in twos, threes, fours, and so on, generating the number sequences through pattern investigations.

Sometimes the children generated the counting sequences spontaneously, and sometimes I initiated the work.

To introduce counting in threes, I gave each child nine Unifix cubes and told them to arrange them in groups of the same size. They all grouped the cubes in threes. Then the children were invited to try a few different ways to count how many cubes they had. One girl recalled a rhyme presented in class some time before and counted, "One little, two little, three little pigs, four little, five little, six little pigs, seven little, eight little, nine little pigs." Some children counted rhythmically, "One, two, **three**, four, five, **six**, seven, eight, **nine**."

All the children liked the rhythmic counting and from then on used it widely in their pattern work. Rhythmic counting of the threes pattern led the children to use the counting sequence, "three, six, nine, twelve … ".

The children's early work on repeating patterns and counting sequences was the basis for an understanding of multiplication and division. It also laid the foundation for more complex counting sequences such as the doubling pattern (1, 2, 4, 8, 16, 32 …).

6.2 Number investigation topics

Suggested topics

The possibilities for number investigation topics are endless. The most common type of topic is simply the investigation of a particular number. Here are some suggested variations which add interest.

- Why is thirty-six an interesting number?
- Is eleven a boring number?
- The answer is ten; what is the question?
- Birds' toes (The children did some library research and found that most birds have four toes on each foot. They focused their further work on the possible arrangements of the four toes.)
- Sharing a blackbird pie (This referred to the nursery rhyme pie with twenty-four blackbirds. It involved the children in working out the many ways a blackbird pie can be divided so that the people eating it get equal shares of pastry and blackbirds. It could be divided into thirds, for example, with eight blackbirds in each slice.)
- Making rectangles with sixty Unifix cubes.
- Why do you think people decided to have sixty minutes in an hour?

Other investigation topics centred on relationships between numbers rather than simply on one number.

- Doubling numbers
- Halving numbers
- Quarters
- Tenths
- Noah's Ark numbers (focusing on even numbers)
- How many legs do animals have? (again, focusing on even numbers)
- Adding odd numbers
- Adding even numbers
- Adding an odd number and an even number
- Adding eight
- Finding the difference between ten and numbers less than ten
- Subtracting two
- Adding four to numbers ending with seven
- Combinations of ten
- Are there any numbers of cubes that can only be made into one rectangle?
- Find some numbers less than zero
- Find some numbers between one and two
- Counting in fours
- Finding as many square numbers as we can
- What might a cubic number be?
- Finding pyramid numbers
- Adding two-digit numbers

Setting a topic

We set the day's topic in an introductory discussion during which the person who suggested the topic explained why he or she wanted that topic investigated, or where the idea had come from, perhaps relating it to previous work.

In the earliest investigations I used the introduction to ask the children to suggest questions which might direct their work. I also suggested materials they might use, or asked the children to think of possible new materials.

6.3 Responding to a topic

As in all investigative work, the children worked on the topics in their own ways, and this enabled them to work at their own levels.

Making a start

If the children were investigating a number, they began by making patterns (ordered arrangements) with the appropriate number of Unifix cubes, in response to questions they set: Is it odd or even? Is it a square number? Is it a triangular number? How many rectangles can I make?

Once they had made patterns with the cubes, the children used a range of materials to record their findings. They made pictures, wrote stories and problems, composed songs, made games and wrote reports and number sentences.

When investigating number relationships, the children learned to approach topics systematically in order to generate patterns. For example, when investigating halving numbers, most children began by halving one, then halving two, and so on.

Making pictures

The children drew and painted their patterns. Another popular way of making pictures of patterns was to print them, using items such as boxes, cotton reels and cardboard rolls dipped in paint.

The children made collage patterns too, mostly from squares of coloured paper, but sometimes using other materials such as paper patty pans or scraps of fabric.

Sometimes a pattern with Unifix cubes would be translated into a picture telling a story. For instance, when we investigated sixteen, one girl grouped her cubes into four fours, painted a picture of four dogs and wrote, "sixteen legs at the vet".

The children liked doubling numbers by painting blobs on one half of a sheet of paper and then folding it and thus printing the blobs onto the other half of the paper. They even made half-blobs by dabbing a tiny bit of paint onto the fold in the middle of the paper. Thus they could show that half of nine was four and a half.

The children found pictures useful for showing number relationships. For instance, they found pictures helpful to show that the sequence of triangular numbers resulted from adding consecutive numbers beginning with one.

When Lisa and Karen added consecutive odd numbers, starting from one, and produced the sequence of square numbers, they made pictures to show how that happened.

When investigating the number eleven, Adam made pictures of candles from coloured paper. He drew ten spots along each candle and he drew one spot on each flame. He used his pictures to build up and demonstrate the "counting in elevens" pattern.

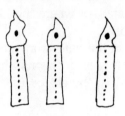

Writing stories

The children wrote stories based on their patterns. Alison made this pattern with nine Unifix cubes and wrote a story.

> nine
> One dog and one cat.
> One mouse and one
> piece of cheese.
> One fox and one
> box.
> One girl and one
> boy.
> And one fluffy rabbit.

Brendan found that ten cubes could be grouped in pairs, and wrote this book.

Ten tanks
There were ten tanks.
2 got blown up. 8 left ...
2 more got blown up. 6 left ...
2 more got blown up. 4 left ...
2 more got blown up. 2 left ...
The last 2 got blown up.

When Jenny made all the possible rectangular arrangements of twenty, she wrote the following story based on Pat Hutchins' *The Doorbell Rang* (Puffin, 1988).

> My friends
> I went out side.
> My friend was there.
> I went to her house.
> Her mum made some biscuits.
> 10 each.
> 2 of my friends came in.
> 5 biscuits each.
> 1 of my Mums friends came in.
> How many biscuits each?

A group of children adopted the idea in Pat Hutchins' story and wrote a play with eighteen pieces of cheese and one, then two, then three, then six, then nine, then eighteen mice to share the cheese.

The next story, based on counting in twos, was so well-liked by the class that the author and her friends made an enlarged copy of it for the class to use.

The secret

I have a secret and no one to tell. Along comes a friend. Four ears to hear the secret. Along comes another friend. Six ears to hear the secret. Along comes another friend. Eight ears to hear the secret. Along comes another friend. Ten ears to hear the secret. Along comes another friend. Twelve ears to hear the secret. Along comes another friend. Fourteen ears to hear the secret. The whole world knows my secret now. It's my birthday!

We made the following book, based on counting in twos, into a "loop story", writing it on sheets of paper stuck together in a continuous roll. We looped it around a curtain rod and it hung down almost to the floor. The children read the story by pulling the looped paper gently around the rod.

Eyes

2 eyes staring, 4 eyes staring, 6 eyes staring, 8 eyes staring, 10 eyes staring, 12 eyes staring, 14 eyes staring, 16 eyes staring, 18 eyes staring, 20 eyes staring … at me reading this story which goes like this …

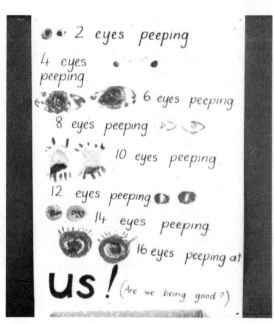

A variation on the "Eyes" story.

A later loop story focused on counting in threes and followed a class trip to a butcher shop.

Sausages

The butcher made lots of sausages. He tied them all in threes. 3 sausages, 6 sausages, 9 sausages, 12 sausages, 15 sausages, 18 sausages … A lot of people came and bought the butcher's sausages. None left! So …

The next story by one of the girls focused on counting in fours.

Frogs
4 frogs. "No more! Please!"
8 frogs. "No more!" "O.K. O.K."
12 frogs. "No more!" "O.K."
16 frogs. "No more! Please!"
20 frogs. "No more! Please!!!"
24 frogs. "Too many frogs!"

The doubling pattern (1, 2, 4, 8, 16, 32 …) was very popular and several stories were based on it.

Twins
Once there was a snake, a beautiful snake. The snake laid an egg. Out of the egg came twins.
Those 2 snakes each laid an egg. Out of each egg came twins. 4 more snakes!
Those 4 snakes each laid an egg. Out of each egg came twins. 8 more snakes!
Those 8 snakes each laid an egg. Out of each egg came twins. 16 more snakes!
Those 16 snakes each laid an egg. Out of each egg came twins. 32 more snakes!
All boys!

Composing songs

Sometimes the children composed songs based on their patterns. They began by determining the number of bars and number of notes to a bar, then wrote the words and composed a percussion accompaniment.

Stacey's "Twelve" song was based on a pattern of three fours, so there were three bars with four notes in each bar.

Hipperty hop

Red kangaroo

I can see you.

Liza's "Twenty-four" song was based on a pattern of four sixes.

I bought a cat one day
And then put it to bed.
It made a great big mess.
I threw it out of bed!

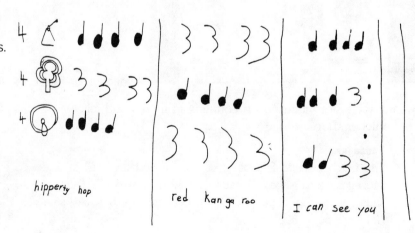

Making games

The children made games based on some of their patterns. They liked to make square numbers into board games that were variations of draughts and chess. Other games they made focused on learning number facts and will be discussed later in the book (see Chapter 7).

Writing problems

Mark drew this problem when he investigated the number ten and found it was a triangular number.

David wrote the following problem when he was studying twenty-four.

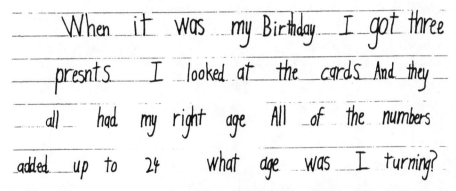

The following book was the result of an investigation of the number of rectangles that could be made with sixty Unifix cubes.

Rectangles of sixty

1 row of ...
2 rows of ...
3 rows of ...
4 rows of ...
5 rows of ...
6 rows of ...
10 rows of ...

The children turned several of their pattern-based stories into problems. This one was based on the doubling pattern.

WHAT COMES NEXT?

1 crocodile in the swamp.

2 crocodiles in the swamp.

4 crocodiles in the swamp.

8 crocodiles in the swamp.

16 crocodiles in the swamp.

32 crocodiles in the swamp.

64 crocodiles in the swamp.

What comes next?

The next problem focused on the sequence of triangular numbers.

BIRDS

1 bird in a cage on Monday.

3 birds in a cage on Tuesday.

6 birds in a cage on Wednesday.

10 birds in a cage on Thursday.

15 birds in a cage on Friday.

How many birds in the cage on Saturday?

The following problem revealed that the writer had a poor understanding of the concept of pattern.

ANIMALS

2 birds

4 cats

3 hippopotamuses

What comes next?

(Her answer was "4 lizards".)

When the writer shared her problem with the class, several children said, "That doesn't make sense". Tim said, "The answer could be six crocodiles because cats eat birds and cats are double the number of birds and crocodiles eat hippopotamuses so you double the number of hippopotamuses." Tim helped the writer to do some more work on the problem.

A fortnight later the same girl produced this problem.

EGGS

There's 2 eggs in the haystack. One's cracked. "Let's take them home." "Go and check the eggs girls." "O.K." "There's 4 eggs. 2's cracked." "We better take them home."
"Go and check the eggs girls." "O.K." "There's 6 eggs. 3's cracked." "Let's take them home."
"There's 8 eggs this morning. Let's tell Mum there's 8." "And 4's cracked."
How many eggs the next day?

Writing reports

The children wrote reports which included word sentences and number sentences.

Some of the earlier reports were poorly focused, such as the following.

Nine

I like nine. It is a lovely number. I love it. It is my favourite number.

Timothy's report on the number twenty-four is a much later piece of work.

Twenty four

24 is not a triangular number. 24 is not a square number either. It is an octagonal number. Half of 24 is 12. Twice as much as 24 is 48. There are 24 hours in a day. You can make lots of different rectangles for 24. 24 is in the fours pattern and the sixes pattern and the twos pattern and the twelves pattern and the threes pattern and the eights pattern and the twenty-fours pattern and the ones pattern. There are 24 eggs in two cartons.

The children wrote extensively about their investigations of number relationships.

Adding 8 to numbers ending with 5

I added 8 to lots of numbers ending with 5. When you add 8 to a number you can add 10 and go back 2. Like if you add 8 to 25 you go to 35 and then 33. So if you add 8 to numbers ending with 5 you get numbers ending with 3. There's a pattern if you start with 5 and go up to 15 and up every 10 more.

$5 + 8 = 13$

$15 + 8 = 23$

$25 + 8 = 33$

$35 + 8 = 43$

$45 + 8 = 53$

I went up to 93.

Halving numbers

All the numbers go odd, even, odd, even and if you get half of an odd number it's something and a half and half of an even number is something and no half. So the pattern is half, 1, 1 and a half, 2, 2 and a half, 3, 3 and a half and it keeps going like that.

Writing number sentences

The children increasingly captioned their pictures and stories with number sentences. They included number sentences in their reports and sometimes chose to write just number sentences as their response to a topic.

The children found number sentences a useful way to record what they found out about number relationships.

David, investigating doubling numbers, wrote the following sequence of number sentences.

1 + 1 = 2	10 + 10 = 20	100 + 100 = 200
2 + 2 = 4	20 + 20 = 40	200 + 200 = 400
4 + 4 = 8	40 + 40 = 80	400 + 400 = 800
8 + 8 = 16	80 + 80 = 160	800 + 800 = 1600
16 + 16 = 32	160 + 160 = 320	1600 + 1600 = 3200
32 + 32 = 64	320 + 320 = 640	3200 + 3200 = 6400

An example: Investigating twenty-five

The work done on the topic "Twenty-five" demonstrates the variety of responses from the class to a set topic.

Erin and Alison made a collage picture of a twenty-five gram packet of Smarties and wrote problems based on there being twenty-five Smarties in the packet. They accompanied their problems with matching number sentences.

Damien and Trevor found items which had a mass of twenty-five grams.

48 MAB ones have a mass of about 25g

6 pencils have a mass of about 25g

25 1g masses have a mass of 25g

5 5g masses have a mass of 25g …

Five children wrote problem books. Four based their problems on patterns of twenty-five. Jacqui based her book on multiples of twenty-five.

---

25 cats, how many legs?
25 flies, how many heads?
25 cows, how many spots if each cow has two spots?

Terri printed twenty-five squares in a square pattern and wrote "25 is a square number". She also painted the sole of one of her feet and printed it five times. "If I had five feet I would have 25 toes. $5 \times 5 = 25$". Michael did the same thing with his hands.

Jackie said, "I want to find out how many threes are in twenty-five." She printed with an oval drink bottle lid and a cotton reel. For each "three" she printed the lid with two cotton reel prints inside it. She printed eight of these and then an empty drink bottle lid print. "25 can be made up of 8 threes and one more," she wrote.

Erica and Liza used plastic replica coins to make a book of number sentences about twenty-five.

How we did it. First we got the plastic money and put them into groups of 25c. Then we wrote number sentences about 25.

5.5 = 25

4.5 + 5.1 = 25

10.2 + 1.5 = 25 …

(Erica and Liza used the dot as a multiplication symbol.)

Craig and David wrote reports. Here is one of them.

Twenty-five is a rectangular number. Twenty-five is a square number. Twenty-five has five fives. Twenty-five is a quarter of one hundred. How many twenty-fives in one thousand? Answer: forty. How many twenty-fives in one hundred? Answer: four. Did you find a pattern in those two last ones? Twenty-five is an eating number. Mostly you find twenty-five grams net and mls on food packets but sometimes you get it on things other than food. At home see how many things there are with twenty-five grams net or mls on and add the twenty-fives up. How much do they add up to?

Tim wrote "A legend about twenty-five".

Ages and ages ago in the Dreamtime an Aborigine went down to the lake and twenty-five cobras jumped out at him. He dodged them. And then he caught twenty-five fish. Then five magpies jumped out at him (which is a fifth of twenty-five). Then one hundred flying fish flew over his head (one hundred is four times twenty-five). And then twelve and a half fish leaped out of the water (twelve and a half is half of twenty-five). Fifty penguins jumped down out of a tree (fifty is double twenty-five). Then he went home to find his children had invited twenty-five children over each (he had two children). And then each child shouted twenty-five times. How many shouts?

Felicia made a game with twenty-five cardboard squares on which she had written combinations of numbers to represent the numbers one to twenty-five. For instance, on the first card she had written ½ of 2, on the second card she wrote 6 – 4, on the third card she wrote, ¼ of 12, and so on. The object of the game was to place the cards in order to make a square.

Tom, Mitchell, Brendan and James investigated rectangular arrangements of twenty-five. They made pictures with pasted paper squares to represent the two rectangles they had made and wrote a report to accompany their pictures.

Four girls each pasted twenty-five coloured paper squares to make a large square and then joined their finished squares together to make a square with one hundred little squares in it. They accompanied their work with number sentences to describe what they had done.

Four children built up the "twenty-fives pattern" (25, 50, 75, 100 ...) and noted the relationships between the numbers.

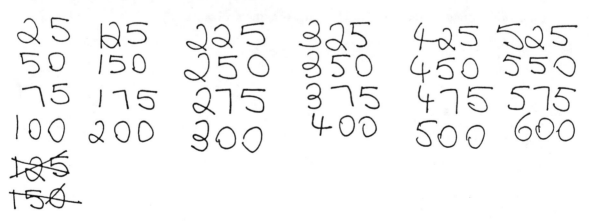

6.4 Following up a topic

Reporting back

We always gathered together after investigative work to discuss the children's findings. This gave further purpose to investigations. Sometimes we translated the children's findings into number sentences.

The children almost always chose what they shared with the class. On only one occasion I intervened because I thought that what Felicia had found would perhaps confuse some of the children. She had been "finding the difference between eight and numbers less than eight". I was standing beside her when she wrote $8 - 9 = -1$ and I asked her to tell me about what she had written. She said, "Well, I know eight minus eight is zero, so eight minus nine means you have to go past zero and it's just one past zero so it must be minus one. Next I'm going to do eight minus ten and that's going to be minus two because it has to be two past zero." I asked Felicia to share her work with a group of nine other children I thought would be able to understand. She did so and three of those children followed her example and spontaneously did some work with negative numbers. They worked together to produce some problems based on negative numbers, and shared the problems with me, rather than with the class.

Following up an investigation

Number investigations were always followed up, even if it was simply in terms of recalling what the children had found out when appropriate to problem-solving. For instance, one of the children wrote a problem which required the addition of all the numbers from one to four. "That's ten," said one of the others. "Remember when we investigated ten and we found out it was one plus two plus three plus four?"

Sometimes we wrote problems together based on the patterns the children had produced in their investigation of a number. When the children were very interested in the doubling sequence 1, 2, 4, 8, 16, 32, 64 ... , I set the following problem.

A ball fell from a wall 16 metres high. It bounced up half as high as it fell. It kept on bouncing and each time it went up half as high as it fell. A girl caught it when it bounced up 1 metre. How many times did it bounce?

Most of the children drew pictures and diagrams to solve the problem.

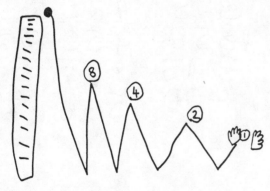

Some children extended the problem when they saw its connection to the sequence of doubling numbers.

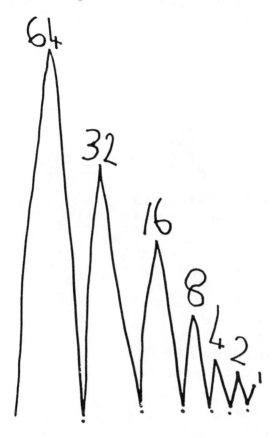

Some follow ups were more extensive. When we studied the number fifteen we followed it up in a few ways. For example, the children considered what they might be doing when they would be 15 years old. After a fascinating discussion in which they showed they had a very clear understanding of the value of fifteen, the children did some writing on the topic. This is what Kate wrote.

When I'm 15

I might have pimples.

My hair might be darker.

I might wear makeup.

I might wear high heels.

I might have a part-time job.

I WILL argue with my parents.

Her delightful illustration showed her Dad asking, "Why did you turn 15 in the first place?"

I asked the children (who were 6 and 7 years old), "When will you be half-way to fifteen?" They figured out that when they were 7½ they would be half-way to 15, so I set them the task of finding the date on which they would be 7½. (See also p.125.)

Following up mistakes

Occasionally a child drew a wrong conclusion as a result of investigative work, as the following example shows.

Doubling numbers

I doubled numbers up to ten.

1 + 1 = 2

2 + 2 = 4

↓

10 + 10 = 20

When you double a number you always get an even number.

When this child shared his work with the class, nobody disputed the conclusion. To overcome this misconception, I asked the children some questions.

I asked, "Do you mean that odd numbers can't be double something?"

"No, because two odd numbers make an even number and two even numbers make an even number."

"If you want to get an odd number you have to put an odd number with an even number and you're not doubling because they're different."

I asked, "What about three? Isn't that double something?"

"No ... Oh, yes. Odd numbers can be double something and a half."

"And halves are double quarters. Any kind of number can be double something."

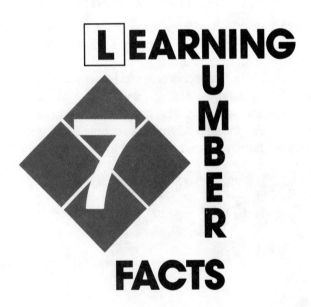

LEARNING NUMBER 7 FACTS

7.1 Mental computation

Why learn number facts?

The children and I discussed the usefulness of memorising number facts such as the combinations of ten. The children said it would make problem solving quicker.

Their learning of number facts grew from the children's investigations of numbers and number relationships.

We sometimes focused on recall of number facts by discussing questions like, "What can you remember about the patterns of twelve?" and "Why is that easy to remember? Can you think of a way to help other children remember that fact?"

We made games to reinforce the learning of number facts. The games were based on the children's investigations. For instance, if they were investigating ten, we would discuss the number combinations they had found and discuss how we could make a game to help the children remember those combinations. Some of the children made games independently of me.

Concrete aids for mental calculation

The children did not learn number facts parrot fashion. I wanted them to refer to concrete and visual models of numbers so that their number fact knowledge was based on an understanding of number relationships.

Fingers were the most convenient concrete model of numbers for children to use. "Finger maths" involved the children investigating ways they could use their fingers to represent numbers. The emphasis was on different ways to represent a number. For instance, eight was represented by four fingers on each hand or by five fingers on one hand and three on the other.

Using their fingers helped the children form appropriate images of numbers which were useful in later mathematics. For example, if children had to double eight, they could hold up five fingers on one hand and three on the other, double the fingers of each hand, then add them. All the children could instantly double five to get ten. Doubling three was easy too. Then they had to add ten and six. (It takes far longer to read this explanation of the method than it took for a child to do the calculation!)

Many children who lack a strongly developed image of numbers, when asked to double eight, answer, "Eighteen". They use the auditory cue, "eight".

To reinforce the children's work with their fingers, several "hands" cut from felt were provided. The children used these to represent numbers, folding down fingers when fewer than a handful were required.

A set of colourful felt "fingernails" was then added to increase the useful-ness of the "hands". The idea for the fingernails came from one of the children who wrote a problem about a girl with variously coloured nails. In the problem, the girl painted her thumbnails green, her index fingernails pink, her middle fingernails gold, her ring fingernails purple, and her little fingernails red. "You can count in twos using coloured fingernails," the writer told the class.

The children used their fingers or the felt fingers and nails to explain what they had found out about numbers.

Stacey said, "I know why six and four is ten. Five fingers and five fingers is ten and you move this thumb near the other hand and it looks like six fingers on one hand and four fingers on the other hand."

David explained, "Eight and two is ten because you've got eight fingers and two thumbs."

Tom said, "You can use your fingers to show how two odd numbers make an even number. You put the two thumbs together and they go off dancing together. The other fingers already have dancing partners."

7.2 Number combinations

Number combination games

The children and I designed several games focused on number combinations.

Frogs

(Number combinations of ten)

Materials:
- 2 "ponds", each with a "lilypad" (made from felt)
- 2 clusters of "frogs' eggs" (made from cardboard)
- 2 "tadpoles" (made from felt, stitched and filled)
- 2 "frogs" (made from felt, stitched and filled)
- A "kiss" (a pair of "lips" made from felt, stitched and filled)
- A die marked 0, 1, 2, 3, 4, 5
- A die marked 5, 6, 7, 8, 9, 10

Procedure:
A pond is placed in front of each player. The two players take turns to throw the 2 dice together. If a combination of 10 is showing, the player collects a clump of frogs' eggs and places it on the pond. The next time that player throws a 10, he or she collects a tadpole, then next a frog (which is put on the lilypad), then finally the kiss (which turns the frog into a prince or princess!) to win.

Planets

❖

(Number combinations of nine)

This game for two players was devised by a group of children. They explained, "We've made up a game to learn the combinations of nine. There are nine planets in our solar system so we could throw a combination of nine and win planets."

Materials:
- 2 "skies" (pieces of black felt with nine holes in each)
- 18 "planets" (table tennis balls painted to represent the planets)
- A die marked 0, 1, 2, 3, 4, 5
- A die marked 4, 5, 6, 7, 8, 9

Procedure:
Each player in turn throws the 2 dice, collecting a planet to place in a hole in their sky if a combination of nine is thrown. The winner is the player who fills his or her sky first.

Spider

❖

(Number combinations of eight)

This game for two players was also suggested by a child.

Materials:

- 16 "spider legs" (black pipecleaners)
- A "spider body" (made from black felt, stitched and filled)
- A die marked 0, 1, 2, 3, 4, 5
- A die marked 3, 4, 5, 6, 7, 8

Procedure:

The players take turns to throw the 2 dice. Each time a combination of 8 is thrown, a spider leg is collected. Once a player has collected 8 legs, the player collects the body on the next throw of an 8 and wins the game.

The children also made similar games to learn the combinations of six (the Bee game) and seven (the Seven Dwarfs game, the Days of the Week game).
    The following two games focus on the difference between numbers.

Pirates

Materials:

- 2 "pirates" (made from coloured modelling clay)
- A "plank" (made from a piece of timber about 50 cm long, marked at 2 cm intervals by lines across it)
- A die marked 0, 1, 2, 3, 4, 5
- A die marked 1, 2, 3, 4, 5, 6

Procedure:

The two players put their pirates at one end of the plank. They take turns to throw the 2 dice. The difference between the numbers showing on the dice indicates the number of steps the player's pirate is to take along the plank. The loser is the first player whose pirate goes over the end of the plank.

Materials:
- "Mr McGregor's garden" (a piece of brown felt, about 25 cm × 30 cm)
- A row of 10 "onions" in the garden (white Unifix cubes)
- A row of 10 "carrots" (orange Unifix cubes)
- A row of 10 "lettuces" (green Unifix cubes)
- A row of 10 "tomatoes" (red Unifix cubes)
- A die marked 0, 1, 2, 3, 4, 5
- A die marked 1, 2, 3, 4, 5, 6

Procedure:
The 2 players (who call themselves Peter Rabbit and Benjamin Bunny) take turns to throw the 2 dice. The difference between the numbers showing on the dice indicates the number of vegetables a player steals from the garden. The play continues until all the vegetables have been stolen. The player who steals the most vegetables is the winner.

Number combination books

We made a series of "How many?" problem books based on number combinations.

On each page, the children had to work out how many objects were hidden under a lift-up flap.

Here is the text of the *Six little ducks* book.

> **Six little ducks**
> Six little ducks that I once knew, some swam away and that left two.
> How many ducks swam away?
> Six little ducks saw some more, some swam away and that left four.
> How many ducks swam away?
> Six little ducks looking at me, some swam away and that left three.
> How many ducks swam away?
> Six little ducks saw a hunter's gun, some swam away and that left one.
> How many ducks swam away?

The seven little kids: This book was based on the traditional children's story, "The Wolf and the Seven Little Kids". On each page some goats were shown and some were hidden. On the lift-up flap covering the hidden goats was written, "How many kids were hiding?".

Eight cherries on a plate: On the first page we wrote this verse.

> Two, four, six, eight,
>
> Eight cherries on a plate,
>
> Count them and calculate
>
> How many Mary ate.

On each of the following pages there was a picture of a plate holding some cherries. On the lift-up flap was the question, "How many cherries did Mary eat?" Under the flap there were cherry stones to represent the eaten cherries. If there were six cherries on the plate, there were two cherry stones under the flap.

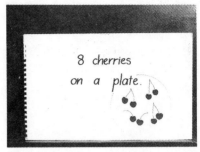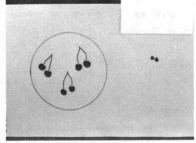

Garfield's nine lives: On the first page we wrote this verse.

A cat has nine lives,
Or so they say.
How many lives
Has Garfield lost today?

Garfield was pictured in various poses on each page. On the flap of each page was written, "How many lives has Garfield lost?". Under each flap the children drew gravestones, each one representing a lost life. If Garfield was pictured six times, three gravestones were under the flap.

The ten little sheep of Little Bo Peep: This book showed a number of sheep on each page and under the lift-up flap the missing sheep were pictured. On the flap on each page was written, "How many sheep has Bo Peep lost?".

7.3 Multiples of numbers

Games based on multiples of numbers

We made several games based on multiples of numbers. These games did not have a winner, so the children could play with them on their own.

The mirror game

Materials:
- Small rectangular mirrors
- Several cards with drawings and directions, for example:
  - A card with 3 fish and the direction, "Make 6 fish".
  - A card with 4 children and the direction, "Make 7 children".
  - A card with 2 pears in one side of a fruit bowl and 1 pear on the other side, and the direction, "Make a bowl with 4 pears".
  - A card with a right-angle triangle and the direction, "Make a square".

Procedure:
The children select a card and follow the direction.

Three little pigs

Materials:
- A "straw house" (a small box covered with straw)
- A "wooden house" (a small box covered in popsticks)
- A "brick house" (a small box covered in rectangles of brown self-adhesive plastic)
- 30 pink counters (to represent pigs)
- A set of cards with directions such as, "Put 12 little pigs in the houses" or "Put 21 little pigs in the houses".

Procedure:
The child selects a card and follows the direction. As for all the games of this type, the children set the rule that the objects — in this case the pigs — would be evenly distributed.

Blackbirds in pies

Materials:
- Some "pies" (cardboard circles, about 30 cm diameter, divided

into segments by lines. On the back of each pie is written a direction such as, "Put 6 blackbirds in this pie.")

- 24 "blackbirds" (made from felt, stitched and filled)

Procedure:
The child selects a pie, reads on the back how many blackbirds are needed, and shares them equally among the pie segments.

Boats on lakes

Materials:
- 5 "lakes" (made from blue cardboard)
- 20 very small toy boats
- A set of cards, giving directions such as, "Put 16 boats on 4 lakes".

Procedure:
The child selects a direction card, takes out the appropriate number of boats and lakes and shares the boats equally among the lakes.

The children devised similar games featuring aeroplanes on runways, cars on roads and straws in cups. I encouraged them to use the games in different ways if they wanted to. Two girls played the "Straws in cups" game and wrote this report on what they did.

Cups

We did not
want to do
what the
card said to
do so we got
the straws and
we got to see
how many we
had so in some
cups we put
10 in each.
We used 6 cups.
we had three
straws left so we
left them. we had 63.

Problems based on multiples of numbers

To help children establish links between number facts and build upon known facts, "if … then … " problems were introduced; for example:

If two threes are six, then what are four threes?
If two fours are eight, then what are four twos?

These questions were usually accompanied by concrete or visual models of the numbers. The children made such questions the subject of books and posters.

WRITTEN NUMBER WORK 8

8.1 Making a start with written recording

Written number work was not a separate entity in the program. The children did not ever sit and "do sums" in the traditional sense. Written number work arose in the context of problem solving, investigations or games.

When investigating numbers, the children found writing number sentences a useful way to record what they had discovered. And when solving problems, they came to recognise the convenience of written calculations.

Sometimes, whilst playing a game, the children drew what they did and captioned their drawings with number sentences.

Early recording

From Kindergarten some children spontaneously wrote about and drew pictures of the mathematics games they played. Their early pictures and writing reflected their involvement in the game rather than the mathematical aspects. For instance, they drew themselves sitting at a table with the game pieces spread out in front of them. Sometimes they wrote captions such as, "I won", or "Me and Stacey played the boats game".

Gradually the children's recording of the games focused on the mathematical aspects.

Liza, playing the "Mirrors" game, selected the card showing two flowers and followed the direction to "Make 4 flowers". This is what she drew.

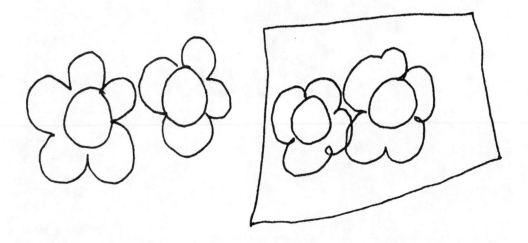

Tasanee played the "Freckly fingers" game and wrote, "I put 10 freckles on the hand". She drew a hand with two freckles on each finger.

Thea played with the "Boats on lakes" game and wrote, "If I put 4 boats on 2 lakes I would have to put 2 boats on each one". (She drew a picture of this.) "And if I put 8 boats on 4 lakes I would have to put 2 on each too." (She drew this also.)

Gradually the children started to use shorthand symbolism to record what they had done.

Adam played with the "Cars on roads" game and put ten cars on five roads so that there were two cars on each road. This is what he drew.

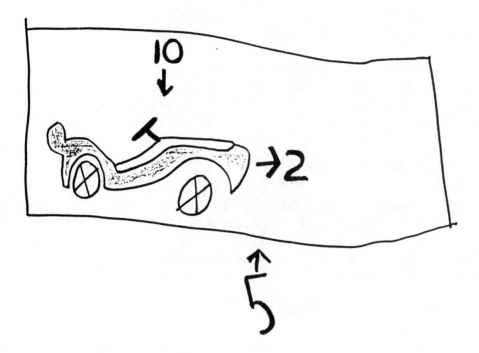

First number sentences

In the first half of Year One many of the children spontaneously wrote number sentences in their investigations. They did not use the standard format or symbolism but invented their own.

When the children investigated "Adding one", they included in their work the following ways of representing adding one to three.

3 add 1 4

3, 1, 4

3 ← 1 is 4

④
1
3

(Erica explained the following representation of adding one by counting up bottom, "1, 2, 3 ... add 1, is 4.")

4
1
3
2
1

8.2 Standard number sentences

Addition sentences

One day, mid-way through Year One, I asked the children what they were learning when they played the "Frogs" game (see p.107). "What are the combinations of ten that you've learned when you've been playing the game?"

I had made some cards with a number from 0 to 10 written on each. Another card had *and* on one side and + on the other. As the children suggested combinations of ten, I put the appropriate cards on the blackboard ledge so that they could read

$$\boxed{4} \quad \boxed{\text{and}} \quad \boxed{6}$$

When all the number pairs had been suggested, I turned over the card with *and* on it to reveal the + sign. The children quickly guessed that the sign was a shorthand way to write "and" when using it with numbers.

The next day each child was asked to write a report on the number combinations of ten. Most of the children wrote a list of number pairs and used the + sign.

Corinne wrote her report in number sentence form.

$$
\begin{aligned}
5 + 5 &\text{ is } 10 \\
7 + 3 &\text{ is } 10 \\
10 + 0 &\text{ is } 10 \\
4 + 6 &\text{ is } 10 \\
70 + 6 &\text{ no} \\
1 + 9 &\text{ is } 10
\end{aligned}
$$

When the children shared their work with the class, I introduced the term by telling them that Corinne had written "number sentences".

All the children started using number sentences in their investigative work. Here are some examples of their early work.

staircases

1 is 1
1 + 2 is 3
1 + 2 + 3 is 6
1 + 2 + 3 + 4 is 10
1 + 2 + 3 + 4 + 5 is 15

Adding 1

1 + 1 is 2
3 + 1 is 4
5 + 1 is 6
7 + 1 is 8
9 + 1 is 10
all even
But! 2 + 1 is 3
4 + 1 is 5

2 + 2 is 4
4 + 4 is 8
8 + 8 is 16
16 + 16 is 32
32 + 32 is 64

Mrs skinner.
it is very.
hard.

Multiplication sentences

The children were particularly interested in regular patterns and many of their number sentences reflected this. For example, when exploring twelve, most children would include among their number sentences:

6 + 6 is 12

4 + 4 + 4 is 12

3 + 3 + 3 + 3 is 12

2 + 2 + 2 + 2 + 2 + 2 is 12

1 + 1 + 1 + 1 + 1 + 1 + 1 + 1 + 1 + 1 + 1 + 1 is 12

Many of the children began to write shorthand versions of these in the forms "2 6 is 12" or "2 6s are 12".

Two children used a dot to separate the first two numbers in these shorthand sentences (2.6 is 12). One explained why she did this by saying, "If you put a dot in between the two and the six it doesn't look like you're saying twenty-six is twelve". The class discussed the use of the dot and all the children chose to use it from then.

Later I introduced the × sign as an alternative to the dot.

The children did not have to conform to a standard format for their written number work. They chose their own ways to write number sentences, as the following work demonstrates.

36

18.2   are in 36

12.3   are in 36

9.4   are in 36

6.6   is   36

7.5 plus 1 is 36

2. 10s is 20

2. 10s + 5 is 25   another   lot of 5 is 30   3.10 + 7 is 37 add 2 more + that is 39 + 1 more is 40 + I put another 10 across and I got 50.

12

a ————— of 12 is 12

6 ————— of 2 is 12

4 ————— of 3 is 12

18

18 is 2.9s

18 is 3.6s

18 is 18.1s

18 is 9.2s

18 is 6.3s

and 18 is 1.18

Division sentences

The children's spontaneous number sentences focused on addition and multiplication. The structure of the written sentences closely matched the children's spoken sentences. This was not the case with division and subtraction. The children did not speak of division and subtraction in sentences readily translated into number and operation symbols.

To help them formally express the subtraction and division facts they were explaining, I drew on the children's own work and the language they used.

Division formed the basis of many of the children's investigations. "I know twenty-four is in the fours pattern. I'm going to find out how many fours it's got". "Let's share twenty-four cubes and see how many we get."

We discussed the ways children began investigating number patterns. Their responses included the following two.

"I see how many ones there are in the number. That's easy because it's the same as the number. Then I see how many twos but not if it's an odd number. Then I see how many threes are in it and I keep going like that."

"I see if it's in the threes pattern or the fours pattern or other patterns."

"How do you do that?" I asked.

"On the bead frame. I count in threes and fours and fives on that."

"Then what do you do?" I asked.

"I count how many threes in it if it's in the threes pattern."

A selection of division problems the children had written was also presented and I asked the children to discuss the steps they took to solve them.

AXOLOTLS

20 axolotl legs in our fishtank. How many axolotls?

DOUGHNUTS

Mum bought 12 doughnuts. How many doughnuts each for me and David and Alison?

In their explanations of how they solved these problems, the children said they started with the number of objects (axolotl legs or doughnuts) and then "counted how many fours there were" or "shared them between three people".

We devised two sentence structures to express these actions:

Twenty, how many fours?

Twelve, shared between three?

Soon afterwards, a pair of children engaged in a "written conversation" when they investigated counting in fives. They took turns to write questions and give answers.

The fives pattern

15 how many 5s? 3

40 how many 5s? 8

60 how many 5s? 12

(and so on)

Written conversations became a popular way of exploring number relationships. The children did not confine their questions to division.

The ÷ sign was introduced later as a shorthand version of "how many" and "shared between".

Subtraction sentences

The children's approaches to subtraction were particularly interesting. Schools usually introduce subtraction as "taking away", yet many real-world subtraction problems do not involve taking away anything.

The children's problems covered the three types of subtraction (finding differences, amending deficiencies and taking away).

In their investigations they described subtraction facts in terms such as, "Four is one less than five" or "Five is one more than four". Usually they wrote these facts as addition sentences:

4 + 1 is 5
5 is 4 + 1

The children did not use the term "take away" in their investigations.

I listened carefully to their discussions and explanations and decided that, when focusing on subtraction, they were generally thinking in terms of the difference between numbers. I took the first step in linking their thinking and talking to the standard expression of subtraction by using the term "difference between" when appropriate.

To follow up an investigation on the number twelve, for instance, I asked, "What's the difference between twelve and ten?"

"Twelve's bigger."

"How much bigger?" I asked.

"Two more."

"Yes," I said, "The difference between twelve and ten is two."

The games "Pirates" and "Mr McGregor's garden" (see pp.109-10), reinforced the children's understanding of "difference between".

I introduced the word "minus" as meaning "the difference between" and the children began using the term in association with the two games and in their investigative work. They said, and wrote in words, sentences such as, "Six minus four is two". Much later I introduced the – sign as shorthand for the word "minus".

The children started writing subtraction sentences in their investigations of numbers. Some investigation topics specifically dealt with subtraction:

- One less than
- Getting smaller
- The difference between ten and numbers less than ten

Subtraction investigations led to the work shown on the next page.

(50)

50 - 0 is 50
60 - 10 is 50
70 - 20 is 50
80 - 30 is 50
90 - 40 is 50
100 - 50 is 50

(50)

50 - 0 is 50
50 - 9 + 9 is 50
50 - 1 + 1 is 50
50 - 2 + 2 is 50
50 - 3 + 3 is 50
50 - 4 + 4 is 50
50 - 5 + 5 is 50
50 - 6 + 6 is 50
50 - 7 + 7 is 50
50 - 8 + 8 is 50

DAVID
getting smaller
18 September
10 - 1 is 9
10 - 1 - 1 8
10 - 1 - 1 - 1 is 7
10 - 1 - 1 - 1 - 1 is 6
10 - 1 - 1 - 1 - 1 - 1 is 5
10 - 1 - 1 - 1 - 1 - 1 - 1 is 4
10 - 1 - 1 - 1 - 1 - 1 - 1 - 1 is 3
10 - 1 - 1 - 1 - 1 - 1 - 1 - 1 - 1 is 2
10 - 1 - 1 - 1 - 1 - 1 - 1 - 1 - 1 - 1 is 1

Sixes

0 F 6 B 6 is 0

(The child wrote this as she worked with a number line. Each sentence begins with zero. F means forward and B means back.)

0 B 6 F 6 is 0
0 F 6 B 3 is 3
0 B 6 F 3 is –3
0 F 6 F 6 is 12
0 B 6 B 6 is –12

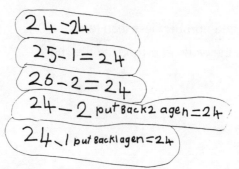

24 = 24
25 - 1 = 24
26 - 2 = 24
24 - 2 put Back 2 agen = 24
24 - 1 put Back 1 agen = 24

The children used the minus sign to represent the three types of subtraction. We discussed its use often. We determined that the three types of subtraction could all be classified as finding the difference between numbers. Sometimes finding the difference between numbers could best be done by taking away; sometimes it was better to add on. For instance, to find the difference between seventy-three and seventy-one, it was better to add on. If finding the difference between seventy-three and seventy-two, it was better to take away.

Using calculators

The children used calculators occasionally in the latter half of Year One and about once a fortnight in Year Two.

In Year One I set calculator investigation topics such as these:

- How can you make a two-digit number on the calculator screen?
- How can you use a calculator to add two numbers?
- How many ways can you use a calculator to add five threes?
- How can you use a calculator to find the difference between two numbers?
- How can you use a calculator to find how many twos are in sixteen?
- How can you change twenty into thirty without clearing the screen?
- How can you change twenty into nineteen without clearing the screen?
- How can you use a calculator to help you count in fives?
- How can you use a calculator to help you count in twos backwards from twenty?
- How can you use a calculator to find some triangular numbers?

As the children investigated the use of calculators, they developed familiarity with the symbols for the four operations. The calculators also introduced the standard symbol for equality to the children. The = sign began appearing in their number sentences soon after the children started using calculators.

In Year Two the children sometimes used calculators when setting and solving problems and when investigating numbers and number relationships. Calculator investigation topics were set as for Year One, for example:

- How can you use a calculator to find half of a number?
- How many ways can you use a calculator to find a quarter of a number?
- How can you use a calculator to find some square numbers?
- How can you change 1245 into 1205 without clearing the screen?

Games to reinforce the meaning of operation symbols

Together we made the following games to reinforce the meaning and use of the subtraction and addition signs.

Rubbish

Materials:
- 2 miniature rubbish bins (about 20 cm high)
- 20 "rubbish parcels" (10 cm-long rolls of newspaper covered with clear self-adhesive plastic)

- 30 "bones" (made from white cardboard)
- A die marked +, +, +, −, −, −
- A die marked 3, 4, 5, 6, 7, 8
- A die marked 10, 10, 10, 20, 20, 20

Procedure:
The two players each have an empty rubbish bin. They take turns to throw the three dice. They add the numbers showing on the two number dice if a plus sign is thrown. They find the difference between the two numbers if a minus sign is showing. They take rubbish parcels (representing "tens") and bones (representing "ones") equal to the total they work out from the dice. Ten bones are exchanged for a rubbish parcel. As a player gets a rubbish parcel it is put into his or her bin. The player who has the most rubbish when all the rubbish parcels are taken is the winner.

Lost Penguins

(We made up this game after the children had researched penguins.)

Materials:
- A game board with a trail of numbered squares leading to a map of Antarctica
- An Emperor Penguin (made from black and white Unifix cubes, to which cardboard feet, plastic eyes and a yellow ribbon around the neck were added)
- An Adelie Penguin (smaller than the Emperor and without the ribbon)

- A die marked 5, 6, 7, 8, 9, 10
- A die marked +, +, +, +, −, −

Procedure:
The players put their penguins on the first square. They take turns to throw the dice and move accordingly. If +9 shows, the player moves forward 9 squares. If −3 shows, the player moves back 3 squares. If a player throws a negative number on the first throw (say −3) the player must get some Unifix cubes (in this case, 3) and put them behind the start to create more squares. The first player to reach Antarctica is the winner.

(I chose the numbers for the dice so that the children would have opportunities to develop strategies for adding large single-digit numbers. The children decided on the number of addition and subtraction signs to put on the second dice. Some interesting work on probability arose from this.)

8.3 The relationship of written recording to problems and investigations

Problems and number sentences

Sometimes we discussed the relationship between number sentences and problems. What number sentence could we write to show how we worked out a given problem? Could we write more than one number sentence to show what we did?

For instance, take the following problem written late in Year One.

POCKET MONEY

I t's not fair. My brother gets three dollars for pocket money and I only get two dollars. How much more does my brother get?

I asked the children to suggest number sentences that described how they worked out the problem.

"I found the difference between three dollars and two dollars so I would write $3 − $2 = $1."

"I said three dollars is one more dollar so I would write $2 + $1 = $3.

Investigations and number sentences

Sometimes we followed up the children's number investigations by writing a series of number sentences representing what the children had found. The children made the suggestions and either I or they did the recording.

When they investigated fifteen, some children made collages or printed patterns to show that fifteen was a triangular number, and to show the rectangles that could be made from fifteen. Some made necklaces with fifteen beads arranged in fives or threes or in the triangular pattern. One pair of children made a pattern they called a chain, with each link made from three paper squares. One boy painted one of his hands and printed it three times on a piece of paper to show that fifteen was made up of three fives. One child halved and quartered fifteen.

The children shared their work at the end of the session and suggested number sentences we could write to describe their findings. I started by asking how they had gone about getting their fifteen Unifix cubes.

Erica said, "I got a ten and five ones." To record this, the children suggested I write $10 + 5 = 15$.

Karen said, "I got two tens and broke off five." The children told me to write $20 - 5 = 15$.

Trevor said, "Me and Tim got ten each and another ten and split it in half." The children suggested two number sentences.

$$\tfrac{1}{2} \text{ of } 30 = 15$$

$$10 + \tfrac{1}{2} \text{ of } 10 = 15$$

Then we looked at the children's patterns and the children dictated number sentences to describe them. To record that fifteen was a triangular number, the children suggested the following sentences.

$$1 + 2 + 3 + 4 + 5 = 15$$

$$5 + 4 + 3 + 2 + 1 = 15$$

To show that fifteen was an odd number the children decided on the following number sentence.

$$7 \times 2 + 1 = 15 \text{ ("Seven twos plus one is fifteen.")}$$

To describe the rectangles that could be made from fifteen, the children suggested the following.

$$3 \times 5 = 15$$

$$5 \times 3 = 15$$

$$15 \times 1 = 15$$

$$1 \times 15 = 15$$

The last sentences recorded the fraction work Damien had done.

$$\tfrac{1}{2} \text{ of } 15 = 7\tfrac{1}{2}$$

$$\tfrac{1}{4} \text{ of } 15 = 3\tfrac{3}{4}$$

8.4 Vertical algorithms

The children began writing vertical algorithms when they found them useful for adding numbers greater than ten (see p.55). They began arranging numbers vertically because they found it a good way to keep the ones together and the tens together (and so on). Later they used vertical algorithms for subtraction.

Vertical addition

When the children became interested in vertical addition, they wrote problems incorporating lists of numbers.

AMERICA'S CUP

One day we went to the America's cup. Before the race we bought:
99 beers
   13 pizzas
   16 hamburgers
They wouldn't let us on the boat after that. How many things did we eat?

The children found vertical algorithms useful for explaining some number relationships which they investigated.

Adding ten to other numbers

When you add ten more to numbers you get another number that ends the same as the first number.

27 +

<u>10</u>

<u>37</u>

One more ten.
No more ones.

Vertical subtraction

The children's favoured subtraction algorithm involved writing the higher number of a pair at the top of a piece of paper and the lower number much further down the page. The children then found the difference by either of two methods.

If all the digits in the lower number were less than the equivalent digits in the higher number the children often found the difference between the ones, between the tens, and so on.

46 –

22

"Two more tens, four more ones, that's twenty-four".

If any of the digits in the lower number were higher than the equivalent digits in the higher number, then the children found the difference by adding on.

53 –

28

"Twenty-eight up to thirty is two, thirty up to fifty-three is twenty-three, that's twenty-three plus two … twenty-five."

Conclusion

At the end of Year Two all the children were competent at using written mathematical computations, and they were adept at mental calculation. So they had achieved the conventional goals of junior primary school mathematics.

The work the children generated, and their very great enthusiasm for mathematics, led them to three other major achievements. They had become mathematically articulate: they were able to describe and explore mathematical ideas using a rich vocabulary of spoken and written words. They were competent at posing and solving a wide range of mathematical problems. And the children had become able mathematical investigators, exploring topics with initiative and confidence.